THIS W

(God's Part, ... Part)

by Charles ❤ Frances Hunter

published by
Hunter Ministries Publishing Company
1600 Townhurst
Houston, Texas 77043

Canadian Office
Hunter Ministries Publishing Company of Canada
P.O. Box 30222, Station B
Calgary, Alberta, Canada T2M 4P1

Scripture quotations are taken from:

The Authorized King James Version (KJV)
The Living Bible, Paraphrased. ©1971 by Tyndale House, Publishers, Wheaton, Illinois. All references not specified are from the Living Bible.

ISBN 0-917726-23-5

TABLE OF CONTENTS

INTRODUCTION

Is it possible to stay "up" all the time?

YES!!!

Is it possible for everyone to stay "up" all the time?

YES!!!

Is it possible for even ME to stay "up" all the time?

YES!!!

How?

READ . . .

THIS WAY UP !

THE DISCOVERY

by Frances

This book can change your entire Christian life!

It can start you going in the right direction so fast, you'll never have time to wonder why you didn't realize these simple little truths long ago!

Are you ready to discover how to keep your faith "up" at all times? Let's go!

Television's what started it all!

Charles and I have exciting times as we prepare for our weekly television programs. However, I nearly fainted one morning when he said to me, "Honey, are you aware of the fact that God does very little in the Christian life and that we have a tremendous amount to do?"

I was shocked! I said, "Charles! You've got to be kidding. That's really sacrilegious. Don't ever say that again, honey, and I certainly hope you'll never say it in public."

Then Charles said, "Come here, Sweetheart. I want you to look at these scriptures, because I believe this is why most people don't have the tremendous excitement they should have in their Christian life. They don't realize that even though God has a part to do, we have a very important part to do also."

I went over to Charles, and we began to examine the scriptures together, and do you know what I discovered? He was right, just like he always is! We began to see that many people are not enjoying the abundant life that Jesus promised because they fail to do the part given to them by God.

Here is the scripture that started it all:

> *For God is at work within you, helping*
> *you want to obey him, and then helping*
> *you do what he wants (Phil. 2:13).*

GOD GIVES US THE . . .

DESIRE . . . (He places it in our hearts)

THE WANT . . .(He creates in us a "want.")

THE OPPORTUNITY . . . (every day)

THE POWER . . . (Holy Spirit)

but he leaves the final decision up to us, because he never takes away from us our choice as a free, moral agent. He never makes a robot out of us.

God works through human beings, empowering us as much as we need and will accept, but letting us forever and ever make our own choices. Once we find out what our part is, and what God's part is, we're on the right road.

Where does it all start?

It starts with salvation!

Who has the first job to do in salvation?

God's part actually is first, because it is the Holy Spirit who convicts us of our sins. Do you remember the misery you went through before you were saved when God's Holy Spirit told you about being a sinner? I did more arguing with God over whether or not I was a sinner than anything else, but the Holy Spirit was relentless. I kept saying, "But, God, look at all those tuna fish sandwiches I made. Look at all those cream cheese sandwiches I made. Look at all the dishes I washed at the church suppers."

God kept saying, "You're a sinner."

I kept saying, "No, I'm not!"

He kept saying, "Yes, you are!"

I kept saying, "No, I'm not!" But God never gave up, and finally one day, I confessed that I was a sinner! At last, I did *my* part!

> *If we confess our sins, he is faithful and*
> *just to forgive us our sins, and to cleanse*
> *us from all unrighteousness (I John 1:9*
> *KJV).*

Then God did his part!

There are two parts to salvation. God's part, which is to remind us of sin, and then our part, which has to be done before anything else can happen. The minute you confess your sins, you activate the very throne of God, because then God has to do his part.

What is God's part? To forgive us of our sins, and to cleanse us of all unrighteousness. God is faithful, because he ALWAYS does his part.

Now you are saved!

Now your sins are forgiven!

Now you are cleansed!

Now your sins are all buried in the deepest sea, never to be rememberd again! Hallelujah! Do you know that if you were saved just five seconds ago, and you said, "Oh, God, did you forgive me of that sin?" God would reply, "What sin?" He would never remember them again!

Now you are washed as white as snow!

Now you are free from all guilt! Glory to God!

Now that we're saved, who has the next part to do? WE DO!!! Why?

> *Therefore if any man be in Christ, he is a new creature: old things are passed away; behold, all things are become new (II Cor. 5:17 KJV).*

We became brand new creatures.

If you are saved, ACT LIKE YOU ARE!

I've seen many people who came to an altar, cried and boo-hooed all over the place, and everyone was really excited because Johnny got saved! Then he walked out the door and continued living like the devil himself.

Did he get saved?

No, he didn't get saved.

He had a great emotional experience, but he sure didn't get saved, because he's still the same old creature.

When I became a Christian, God put in my heart a hungering and thirsting for the word of God that has never been satisfied, and I know will never be satisfied until the day I see him face to face! He started me off differently than most people, because I started reading the Bible in the Epistles, whereas most people start in the Gospels. Interestingly enough, these are the chapters that give the guidelines on how to live the Christian life.

A lot of people don't realize they have a great responsibility after they're saved. They think they are the same old creatures, with the same old nasty sins. Leave them behind! That's YOUR part in the Christian life!

OUR PART

Let me say this, then, speaking for the Lord: Live no longer as the unsaved do, for they are blinded and confused. Their closed hearts are full of darkness; they are far away from the life of God because they have shut their minds against him, and they cannot understand his ways.

They don't care anymore about right and wrong and have given themselves over to impure ways. They stop at nothing, being driven by their evil minds and reckless lusts.

But that isn't the way Christ taught you!

If you have really heard his voice and learned from him the truths concerning himself, then throw off your old evil nature — the old you that was a partner in your evil ways — rotten through and through, full of lust and sham (Ephesians 4:17-22).

Who has to throw off the old evil nature?
WE DO!
Is God going to do it for you?
No, he'll give you the desire, the want, the opportunity and the power, but he leaves the actual shedding

of your old nature up to you. We're the one who has to throw off that old evil nature, bury it, and not dig it up again!

MORE FOR US

Now your attitudes and thoughts must all be constantly changing for the better.
Yes, you must be a new and different person, holy and good. Clothe yourself with this new nature (Ephesians 4:23,24).

Do you like to have a new dress or a new suit occasionally? I do, and so does Charles. I look upon salvation as God saying to me, "Frances, I want you to go to the world's most expensive fabric shop. Don't worry about getting there, because I'll translate you at no cost. I want you to get enough material to make you a completely new outfit. Select the most beautiful fabric you can find, and don't worry about the price, because it's already paid for. The only requirements are that it be white, sparkling, and without a single spot or blemish or wrinkle. Get all you need, and then take it to the world's best dressmaker. He'll make a dress for you that fits you perfectly; and it won't fit anyone else but you. The sleeves will be just the right length; they won't be one-quarter inch too long, or too short. The dress will be the right length, not even an eighth of an inch too short or long. The waistline will be perfect. You can raise your arms and worship me, and there won't be any binding in the dress. You won't have to yank on it to pull it down after you've praised me!"

Wouldn't it be exciting to have a dress made like that at no cost? Well, God offered it, so I got the material, and then gave it to the world's best dressmaker, who is Jesus, and he fashioned it into my robes of righteousness. He gave it back to God, who put it in a beautiful big box and wrapped it with sparkling paper, like the glitter of a million stars. Then he tied it with a wide red bow — the blood of Jesus Christ, and gave it to me!

Who has to put on their robes of righteousness?

WE DO!

Whose part is that?

That's our part.

Is God going to put it on you?

No!

Is God going to force you to put it on?

No!

You, by your own free will, have to reach into that box and take out that beautiful new outfit and put it on yourself. That's your part. God does his part, because he gives it to you through the blood of Jesus Christ. Now it's YOUR responsibility to put it on.

Maybe I could say it another way that would make it easier to understand. I took a shower this morning. Would you believe when I got out of the shower that I was standing there stark naked without any clothes on at all? Sure you would. That's not hard to believe at all. That's exactly the way you are when you're saved. You are standing before God stark naked — nothing left against you, nothing that he could even chide you for. (See Col. 1:22.) That's what the word of God says. Then he gives you this brand new, beautiful outfit; the most beautiful outfit you've ever had in your entire life, but YOU have to put it on.

Would you believe that after I took my shower and stood there stark naked this morning, I had to put on my own clothes? Of course you would. Do you think God put them on me? No, he didn't. I had to put them on myself.

The same thing is true with that beautiful new nature God has given you. YOU have to put it on. God will never hold you down and force you to put it on. He leaves that up to you.

Some people throw the box in a corner, because there are a few things they want to hang onto in life. Not big sins, just LITTLE sins, feeling that when they're ready to "give them up," then, they'll put on the robes of righteousness.

In the meantime, what happens to the robes of righteousness? They lie in the corner, get mildewed and wrinkled, and no longer are without a single spot or blemish or wrinkle.

Who has to put on the new nature?

WE DO!

Is God going to put it on you?

No, that's your responsibility.

Some people try to put the new outfit on top of the old nature, without first "throwing off" the old nature. That's about the same thing as a bride walking down the aisle in a beautiful, flowing white gown with dirty blue jeans underneath! God will give you the desire, the want, the opportunity and the power, but he leaves the final action up to you.

MORE OF OUR PART

> *Stop lying to each other; tell the truth, for we are parts of each other and when we lie to each other we are hurting ourselves (Eph. 4:25).*

Christians don't lie, do they? Or do they? I've heard Christians say, "I don't swear, I don't drink, I don't smoke, I don't dance, I don't do anything. I've got to do something to let off steam, so I always drive fast." Really? Then something must be wrong with your Christian life.

Did you know that you can lie just by the inflection in your voice?

I talk to a lot of policemen and patrolmen when they come to our services. I have asked many of them what type of person they stop the most. The reply is always the same, "The ones who have the car pasted up with signs which say HONK IF YOU LOVE JESUS (a better one says TITHE IF YOU LOVE JESUS, ANY FOOL CAN HONK); ONE WAY, JESUS!; IF YOU SEE THIS CAR WITHOUT A DRIVER, YOU MAY HAVE IT, I'VE RAPTURED."

Here is a typical example! A patrolman walks up to the side of the car, and a pretty lady, young or old, looks out the window, blinks her long eyelashes, and says, "Officer, was I doing something wrong?" She knows very well she was speeding!

But the tone of her voice is a lie.

Did you ever "watch and pray?"

Watch the rear-view mirror, and pray that you didn't get caught? That's what a lot of Christians do.

The officer says, "I'm very sorry, but I'm going to have to give you a ticket for going 45 miles per hour in a 40-mile zone. She says, "Officer, I wasn't going 45. I'm a Christian, and I wouldn't speed. I was only going 37. I just looked at my speedometer!"

The officer says, "But we clocked you on radar."

She says, "But officer, look at this old car. You know it wouldn't go that fast!"

Did you ever go through a red light and NOT know it? Of course not. It may have been an accident, but you KNEW it. And yet when the policeman stops you, you say, "Now, officer, what did I do?"

We've got the best policeman in the world, and he doesn't give us tickets. He just keeps a beautiful, loving eye on us so that we don't get them. I never worry about those blinker lights coming up behind me, because God always has his eye on my speedometer, and he's the one I'm concerned about. If I get even one mile over the speed limit, I look up and say, "Whoops, Lord, pardon me," and I bring it right down to the speed limit, or a little below, because God knows. God knows our hearts, too, and he knows whether or not we willfully and deliberately speed.

Just in case you think I never had a problem with lying, do you know where God really nailed me? I was standing in a pulpit in Ohio teaching this subject and when I got to the part where I asked the audience if they thought Christians lied, I waited for their response, but God was the one who responded. He said, "Fat Christians are the biggest liars of all, and you're a FAT Christian!" I could hardly believe my ears, but it was true, and that was the thing that helped to start me on the downward path, weight-wise. Do you have the correct weight on your driver's license.

Just to help you out, here were some of my fibs and facts:

FIB: "I can't understand why I gain weight. I eat like a bird."

FACT: A 500 pound bird.

FIB: "I must have a glandular problem."

FACT: Very few have a glandular problem.

God reminded me of this fact in a spectacular way. Many years ago, the doctors gave me two months to live. I had Addison's disease and myxedema, both fatal diseases. For about ten years the doctors gave me nineteen grains of thyroid every day to keep me alive, and with enough of that to shake a person off their bones, I would fall asleep in a chair and onto the floor, and sometimes sleep for three days. The day I was saved, God healed me, and I've never taken even a quarter-grain of thyroid since that glorious day! Thank you, Jesus! God asked me that day, "Did you forget I healed you?"

FIB: "He eats a lot more than I do. I don't know why I gain weight!"

FACT: At mealtime, but you should see me in between meals!

God reminded me of the six desserts I used to make, two of which went into the refrigerator for supper, and four into my stomach before Charles got home!

The day I really got honest with myself and said I was fat because I ate too much was the day of real awakening in my life. If you've got this problem, ask Jesus to sit across the table from you and watch with compassion, not with condemnation, every bite you eat.

I saw a lady in the store the other day and she commented on the fact that I had lost weight. Then she asked, "How did you do it?" I told her we have a little motto in our house which says, "It looks better on the plate than it does on me!"

She said, "Do you know what my problem is? My problem must be glandular, because I don't eat a thing. I just eat one meal a day." All I could think of was the scripture: *"Stop lying to each other; tell the truth, for we are parts of each other, and when we lie to each other we are hurting ourselves."*

Now, you do YOUR PART. If you really want to lose weight, ask God to help you. Ask him to give you wisdom and knowledge as to what to eat; then, ask God's Holy Spirit to give you obedience. When the Holy Spirit says to you as he slaps your hand, "Get your hand out of that cookie jar," listen to what he says and be obedient.

Who has to stop lying?

WE DO!

Is God going to make you do it?

No, he'll give you the desire, the want, the opportunity and the power, but as always, he leaves the final decision up to you.

Can you think of some areas in your life where you could be a little more truthful? WOW!

MORE OF OUR PART *(by Charles)*

Have you ever been angry with anyone since you became a Christain?

> *If you are angry, don't sin by nursing your grudge. Don't let the sun go down with you still angry – get over it quickly; for when you are angry you give a mighty foothold to the devil (Eph. 4:26).*

What did you do when you got angry? Did you get over it quickly, or . . .?

All sins start with a thought in your mind, and each thought develops into attitudes or other sins. Anger is one of those sins.

It all started with Satan in heaven. He wanted to be equal with God. This was a selfish attitude of trying to please himself. When God threw him out of heaven like a bolt of lightning, he became the prince of this earth and placed into all mankind, starting with Eve, a desire to please self. Wrong attitudes always point to self!

God's laws are all perfect, so God doesn't need to amend them or modify them to meet changing conditions of the world or changes in our relationship to him. Obedience of his laws works FOR us; disobedience works AGAINST us. The law of gravity will always work whether we are Christian or not. If we fall off a tall building, we can expect to be killed when we hit the ground. God isn't cruel to us when we hit the ground and die — we have violated a law, and anytime we violate a law of God, we can expect to suffer the consequences of disobedience. Anytime we obey his laws, we can expect to benefit or be blessed.

If we harbor anger, the law of God tells us that we give a mighty foothold to the devil.

God gives a similar law in Galatians 5:17-21:

> *These two forces within us are constantly fighting each other to win control over us, and our wishes are never free from their pressures.*
>
> *When you are guided by the Holy Spirit you need no longer force yourself to obey Jewish laws.*
>
> *But when you follow your own wrong inclinations your lives will produce these evil results: impure thoughts, eagerness for lustful pleasure, idolatry, spiritism (that is, encouraging the activity of*

*demons), hatred and fighting, jealousy
and anger, constant effort to get the best
for yourself, complaints and criticisms,
the feeling that everyone else is wrong
except those in your own little group —
and there will be wrong doctrine, envy,
murder, drunkenness, wild parties, and
all that sort of thing. Let me tell you
again as I have before, that anyone living
that sort of life will not inherit the
kingdom of God.*

The root of a sin, or disobedience to God's laws, starts
with a thought, then becomes an attitude or act. The
devil knows about these thoughts and he starts to work
to do what he wants most on earth — to get a mighty
foothold on your mind. If the devil has your mind, he
has YOU! That's why he works on your mind. His
work is done by bodiless, powerful creatures called evil
spirits or demons. These creatures cannot be seen by
humans, but they can have a mighty influence on our
lives.

*Last of all I want to remind you that
your strength must come from the
Lord's mighty power within you. Put on
all of God's armor so that you will be
able to stand safe against all strategies
and tricks of Satan. For we are not
fighting against people made of flesh and
blood, but against persons without
bodies — the evil rulers of the unseen
world, those mighty satanic beings and
great evil princes of darkness who rule
this world; and against huge numbers of
wicked spirits in the spirit world (Eph.
6:10-12).*

As soon as thoughts start to form in our minds which will make us contemplate breaking a law of God or sinning against him, the devil sends an evil spirit or demon to try to get Jesus out of our lives, or to keep him from coming into our lives. The devil wants control of our lives, our minds, and ultimately our spirits and souls. He wants to destroy us. But God wants us to have eternal life.

Let's assume that anger is the troublemaker in our lives. Since I don't want to point at you, I will use myself in an example. Of course, since I am perfect(???!!!) I'll use a hypothetical situation.

Let's assume that Frances and I had an exciting meeting at our home last night and we enjoyed seeing God heal the sick, save souls, and baptize people with the Holy Spirit. We didn't get to bed until two o'clock this morning. That's a violation of God's law in itself, because the Bible tells us to get plenty of rest. We cheat our employers if we go to work with our bodies exhausted, and God isn't pleased with that.

The alarm goes off at six o'clock this morning and I groan at the thought of getting my tired body out of bed. With full-sized bags under my half-closed eyes, I struggle to get shaved and dressed. Frances pulls herself out of bed and staggers to the kitchen to cook breakfast. I get to the table and discover the toast is burned, the eggs are cold and just about everything is wrong. In this case (hypothetical, of course), we snap at each other a few times and finally I rush off to work and peck her on the cheek, instead of my usual 3,000 kisses.

My boss hates people who get to work late, and sure enough I rush in thirteen seconds late, and wouldn't you know it — there he stands, looking at his watch! That makes me so mad! I saw him leave at two o'clock yesterday to play golf, and the old grouch wants me to always be right on time. And that guy that's always trying to get me in trouble, snickers at me as I rush past his desk. I'm going to "get" him one of these days, because he makes me so mad. All day long, everything goes wrong, and I'm about to bust — I'm so fed up with it all!

Finally quitting time is here and I call Frances to tell her I'm leaving so we can eat supper early tonight. Just as I start to leave, that guy who's been bugging me makes a cutting remark! I'm so mad I could hit him right in the face, but I don't have time to get into an argument with him so I keep going. As I go out the door, I snag my new suit! When I get to the car I find a flat tire, and get all dirty and sweaty and hot changing it! Finally I'm on the freeway starting home. It's about 100 degrees, it's raining and sultry, my air conditioner stops working and I'm getting madder by the minute! And wouldn't you know it, a car stalls in the single lane leading off the freeway, and blocks traffic for half-a-mile. He could have had that car repaired two weeks ago, but he deliberately let it break down just to delay me! I get madder and madder and hotter and hotter. It's a wonder I don't have a heart attack and it would all be his fault!

Meanwhile, back at the house....

Frances hasn't had such a good day either. Remember, she was tired at the beginning of the day and it started out all wrong, too (in this hypothetical case). We had four "hypothetical" kids who woke up feeling sick with runny noses. They didn't want to eat, but Frances insisted and ... whoops, there went a glass of milk all over the table! They threw wet cereal at each

other and what a mess they made. Finally, Frances put
them back to bed, and mopped up the floor. Just when
she finished, they came back again and knocked over a
jar of honey and broke it! What a mess! Frances was
getting madder (hypothetically) by the minute. She
finally got their sticky clothes off and put them (the
clothes) in the washer. Just as the water gushed into
the machine, the motor burned out. She called the
repairman, and he rudely said, "No, mam, I can't get
there for about two weeks, sorry." He wasn't sorry a
bit — he just didn't want to work. It made her so mad.
Well, the day kept going like that until finally it was
time for me to get home.

Now observe the scene. These two angry monsters
are about to come together just before sundown. You
do know that it's perfectly permissible to be mean and
bad tempered with the ones you love the most, don't
you? That's the devil's law and lie!

But God always does his part! Knowing that it was
almost sundown and we hadn't had time to get over
being angry with each other, God held the sun up for
an extra thirty minutes!!!

NO, HE DIDN'T! God's laws always work perfectly,
and the sun goes down right on schedule every day. He
says, *"don't let the sun go down with you still angry"*
(Eph. 4:26).

But I didn't obey God's laws. I was thinking about
all the people who had done me wrong all day and was
really angry. Just as the sun went over the horizon, I
was giving Frances a piece of my mind and griping
about what went on at the office all day.

Suppertime came and I was mean to the kids, and
angrily told them to get to bed without finishing their

supper. I went into the TV room and fell into a chair to try to get this all off my mind. I pouted and felt sorry for myself and kept thinking about what that guy at the office said to me on the way out. Anger kept getting worse and worse as I harbored it in my mind.

Finally, Jesus came by about ten o'clock. Jesus always has the answer and this was no exception.

I know that just because you stay angry, you are not possessed by a demon. But I do believe that when you disobey God's law and let the sun go down on your anger, the devil sees an opportunity and sends a demon your way to attack you. They can do a lot of things to make you get mad. They can cause things to happen which will irritate you. The story of Job in the Bible is an example of this.

So in this hypothetical case, let's assume that the devil sent a spirit of anger to get Jesus off the throne of my life.

Jesus gives a parable about this, so let's assume this is just for me at ten o'clock at night after this irritating day of anger.

> *This evil nation is like a man possessed by a demon. For if the demon leaves, it goes into the deserts for a while, seeking rest but finding none. Then it says, "I will return to the man (Charles) I came from." So it returns and finds the man's heart clean but empty! Then the demon finds seven other spirits more evil than itself, and all enter the man (Charles) and live in him. And so he is worse off than before (Matthew 12:43-45).*

I read the word of God. Anger leaves me, and I am clean, but empty. The Bible says what God makes clean is clean indeed. I am pure and spotless because the demon is gone. How beautiful this is. The demon of anger goes out looking for a place to rest and doesn't find one, so it comes back and looks into me. I can imagine its eyes (if it has any) got big as it looked in and said, "Wow-e-e! Look at that house I used to live in! It's clean and empty, and doesn't even have a 'for rent' sign on it." The demon gets excited and runs off to get its enemies (the devil has no friends).

In the meantime, I am happy to be rid of this anger. I kiss Frances 3,000 times and tell her how very sorry I am for being so mean and bad-tempered and ask her to forgive me. Finally, off to bed we go, loving Jesus and each other, happy like we always are. How good it is to relax with my mind free from sin and anger. How great it is going to be to get a long night of rest. I stretch and yawn and am just about to drop off to sleep when my mind begins to wander.

That guy at the office makes me so mad! When I get to the office tomorrow morning I'm going to get even with him! I keep thinking about him and don't even realize that two hours have passed and I'm still tossing and turning. Finally I drop off into a troubled sleep.

When morning comes, I jump out of bed and say, "Jesus, let me love you more!"

No, I don't.

For as he thinketh in his heart, so is he (Prov 23:7 KJV).

The first thought that comes to my mind is, "Wait til I get to the office. I'm going to get him! I can't stand the looks of him. All he does is sit around thinking of ways to get me into trouble with the boss." I resent . . .

RESENTMENT . . . There's one of those demons worse than the first, just like Jesus said would happen!

Every time I think about how he must have schemed to hurt me in my job, I hate . . .

HATE . . . There's another of the seven worse than the first!

"And he probably kept me from getting that promotion three months ago. I deserved it more than he did!" I get so JEALOUS . . .

JEALOUSY . . . Whoops, there's another of the seven demons.

The more I think about him, the more my imagination runs away, and the more I can think of ways he has probably done me wrong, and I get so bit-t-e-r . . .

BITTERNESS . . . There's another demon!

Then the Spirit of God reminds me that all these are worse than harboring anger and they have come because I kept thinking thoughts of anger, resentment, jealousy, and bitterness. I know what the word of God says, and the Spirit convicts me, and I begin to feel sorry for myself . . . SELF PITY!

SELF PITY . . . Caught again in another worse than the first.

I try to get self pity out of my mind and I feel sad ...

GRIEF! There I go again!

Well, I wonder if even God loves me because it seems like no one else does, and I feel like everyone has turned against me . . .

LONELINESS! There's another of those demons attacking me.

Suddenly I realize that because I violated one simple law and let the sun go down with me still angry, I have allowed seven spirits more evil than the first to enter into me, and I am worse off than before!

Did you notice that all eight of those attitudes, causing activities of demons which give a mighty foothold to the devil, were directed to me . . . to SELF?

Jesus says, *"If any man will come after me, let him deny himself, and take up his cross daily, and follow me" (Luke 9:23).*

Jesus didn't take up his cross to carry a burden or to feel sorry for himself. He took up his cross to die. That's what he requires of us if we are to follow him — to die to our own desires, to self, and do what he did. Jesus only thought of others, to help them find eternal life with God. And that is what he wants us to do.

Whose part was it to die?

It was Jesus' part.

God didn't die.

Jesus had to do that to carry out his part of the plan of salvation.

We have to die to ourself — that's our part.

God doesn't have to die to himself.

He has already done his part.

How, then, can we get out of this predicament we are in?

Let's assume we are watching a television set, one that has a dial to change channels, not a push-button type. Let's assume we are watching channel 12 (no reflection on your channel 12). We have just snuggled back in our easy chair and settled down for a comfortable evening of enjoyment. The story starts off with two businessmen talking over plans to make a big move in their plant. They are both excited about what they are planning, but one of them has a little different idea about how to go about it than the other. They begin to insist that each is right, and before you know it, they are arguing!

"Charles, the Bible says not to argue! It says that what you think in your heart you become." That's the Holy Spirit reminding me of the thoughts I've allowed to enter my mind.

"Yes, Father. Thank you for reminding me that I was about to get caught in what would lead to anger, and you know my weakness."

So, being led by the Spirit, I change my dial to channel 11. That's better, and I feel good because I have obeyed the voice of the Holy Spirit, warning me about what I was thinking.

On channel 11 is a western story where two Texans are about to come around the corner and meet. They are both talking to themselves, and saying, "I hate him and I'm gonna plug him!"

"Watch it, Charles. Remember the way you got to thinking about hate."

"Yes, Father . . . thank you for not letting me get caught again."

Obediently, I turn the dial to channel 10 and start watching a totally different story. This one is about the beautiful blond secretary who is working so hard for her boss that she is willing to stay overtime to help him. Of course, she has to freshen up a bit and put on some special perfume just as the rest of the staff leave the office. Meanwhile back home, his lovely wife is preparing dinner for his arrival. About seven o'clock she begins to wonder why he hasn't come home. She gets to thinking, "He keeps telling me the work is stacking up at the office so much that he has to work overtime. I saw his secretary the other day. I think she's what is stacking up. I wonder ...."

"Charles, remember what you put into your mind is what you become." "Yes, I know, Father, but you know I don't have a jealous bone in my body. And besides, this is so farfetched that no one would ever get jealous thoughts watching a simple story like this. . . . I wonder if that really was the television repairman that I saw leaving last night just as I drove up to the house."

The way to stop getting into these thought-traps is simple! Let's turn our dial back to where we started, to channel 12. Instead of turning it to the left to channel 11 when the Holy Spirit reminds us that we are putting wrong thoughts into our minds, let's turn it to the right. That's channel 13, the 13th chapter of I Corinthians, which is the Love Chapter of the Bible.

Now, let's find what the Bible has to say about how to operate our TV dial.

Philippians 4:8,9 says: *"Fix your thoughts on what is true and good and right."*

Who is to fix their thoughts? We are! God's thoughts don't need fixing.

"Think about things" . . . Who is to think?

> *(YOU) think about things that are pure and lovely, and (YOU) dwell on the fine, good things in others. (YOU) think about all you can praise God for and be glad about. (YOU) keep putting into practice all you learned from me and saw me doing, and the God of peace will be with you.*

THAT'S GOD, THE GOD OF PEACE, WHO WILL
BE WITH YOU! He will do his part, if we do ours.

When I discovered this beautiful way of changing my
thoughts, I thought I had the solution to the problem
of my mind wandering into thoughts that were not
pleasing to God. But I discovered that when I turned
my dial; turned my mind away from thinking about
that guy at the office, I had formed such a habit of
thinking wrong that my TV dial had corroded, and it
was harder to change my thoughts than I thought it
would be. My mind-dial kept going right back to
thinking about what he had done to make me angry. I
had to get both hands on the dial and twist hard to try
to get my mind off the subject. Then, I got some Holy
Spirit oil and put on it, and kept moving it toward the
fine, good things in the one I was mad at, until God's
Spirit won over my mind.

> *If you (Charles) are angry, don't (YOU)*
> *sin by nursing your grudge. Don't (YOU)*
> *let the sun go down with you still angry*
> *— (YOU) get over it quickly; for when*
> *you (YOU, Charles) are angry you give a*
> *mighty   foothold   to   the   devil (Eph.*
> *4:26).*

Who's part is it to get over being angry?
OUR PART!

God will give the want, the desire, the opportunity
and the power, but he leaves the final decision up to
us.

STILL MORE OF OUR PART *(Frances again)*

> *If anyone is stealing he must stop it and*
> *begin using those hands of his for honest*

> *work so he can give to others in need*
> *(Eph. 4:28).*

Christians don't steal, do they? Or do they? As Christians, we all say, "I wouldn't steal." Whether we realize it or not, we steal in subtle sorts of ways, and are robbing God. In Malachi 3:8 it asks, *"Will a man rob God?"* Yes, he will . . . we rob God by not giving him our tithes and offerings, but do you know how else we can rob God?

I read in the Christian Life magazine, January 1975 issue, that "if you are quite average, then the probability is that you read one book a year, 57 magazine articles, and spend 1,200 hours watching television." Break that down monthly and you'll find that's about 100 hours a month, or roughly, 25 hours a week, which is a little more than three hours a day watching TV!

If you spend three hours a day watching television, you are stealing from God if you don't give God adequate time in his word and in meditating on him instead. The word of God says that we should have as much interest in the things of this world as a dead person does (Col. 3:3), so it's possible to steal *time* from God.

Do you ever spend time gossiping on the telephone? Wouldn't that time be better spent leading someone to Jesus? Wouldn't it be better spent at a Bible study? You can rob God in many little ways by just not making good use of your time.

WHO HAS TO STOP STEALING?

WE DO!!!

Remember, God will give us the desire, the want, the opportunity and the power, but he still leaves that big decision up to us!

MORE AND MORE OF OUR PART

Don't use bad language. Say only what is
good and helpful to those you are talk-
ing to, and what will give them a
blessing (Eph. 4:29).

Christians don't use bad language. Or do they?
Let's find out.

I used to have a shocking vocabulary before I became
a Christian. Every other word was a real "good" swear
word. Then I met Jesus, and he really cleaned up my
mouth. From the day I accepted Jesus as my Savior
and Lord, not a swear word has ever crossed my lips,
nor has a dirty joke ever entered my mind. Jesus is still
in the transforming business!

Charles' father was saved when Charles was about
eight years old. I only met his father one time, and that
was shortly before he died. He was in a coma, but
Charles managed to communicate to him that I was
there. He came out of the coma long enough to say,
"Once I was a sinner . . . ," then he slipped back into
the coma. After a long wait, he weakly said, "Then I
got saved!"

It was obvious what was on his mind when he died,
but it wasn't always that way. I understand he had
quite a vocabulary too, and he used it all the time. But
when he met Jesus, God really cleaned up his mouth,
and he didn't swear anymore.

One day he was out fixing a tire on an old Model T
Ford. He hit his finger and said, "Oh, shoot!" Poppa
kept working on the tire, and before long he skinned
his knuckle and again he said, "Oh, shoot!" Shortly

after that he said it the third time, when Momma Hunter, who is a saint if I ever saw one, looked over at Poppa and said, "Poppa, you didn't quit cussing. You just changed words. You're 'shoot-cussin' now."

Did you ever do any 'shoot-cussin'? One of my favorites, when Charles and I were married was, "Oh, my goodness." One day Charles said to me, "Do you know what the Bible has to say about your goodness? It says your goodness is as filthy rags so quit bragging about it!" Well, that ended my saying that!

Did you ever say any of the following:

Oh, golly!

Oh, heck!

Oh, gosh!

Oh, darn! Think of what the sinner says, and see if you aren't just trying to clean up his vocabulary! How many other things can you think of that you say that would come under the heading of 'shoot-cussin'?

They say that when a criminal decides to take an alias, he usually uses the same initials as his name. In other words, where my name is Frances Hunter, if I were to take an alias, I would probably become Florence Hinklestein. I would still retain the same initials F.H.

Christians do the same thing. Have you ever said, "jeepers creepers," or "jiminy crickets?" Did you see those two initials? "J.C." Jesus Christ is a favorite expression of sinners using the Lord's name in vain. Sometimes what we try to do is to see how close we can stay to our sinning friends and make them comfortable while we're trying to counterfeit Satan's language. We clean up the words a little bit and decide it's all right to use them.

Think of the attitude that makes you say those little shoot-cussin' words. Then let's clean that attitude up, and be a little more careful in our selection of words.

WHO HAS TO STOP USING THE BAD LANGUAGE?

WE DO!!!

Will God stop you?

No!

God will give you the desire, the want, the opportunity and the power, but he leaves that final decision to stop up to you.

May I pray for you right now? "Father, I pray that your Holy Spirit will remind my brother (or sister) of all their 'shoot-cussin' expressions for the next seven days. Thank you, Father, for making us conscious of what we say!"

THERE'S MORE ON OUR PART

Don't cause the Holy Spirit sorrow by the way you live. Remember, he is the one who marks you to be present on that day when salvation from sin will be complete (Eph. 4:30).

And then Ephesians ends with a wonderful challenge to us!

Stop being mean, bad-tempered and angry. Quarreling, harsh words, and dislike of others should have no place in your lives. Instead, be kind to each other, tender-hearted, forgiving one another, just as God has forgiven you

*because you belong to Christ (Eph.
4:31,32).*

Have you ever been mean, bad-tempered and angry? Have you ever quarreled with some one, or had harsh words with someone since you became a Christian?

Have you ever disliked someone?

Have you ever gossiped?

Before I became a Christian, I loved to gossip. Somebody would come in and tell me something. Then they'd say, "Now, don't tell anybody." (That's the fastest way to get something circulated that I know of!) Do you know what "don't tell anybody" means? That means, "Get on the telephone and call everyone that you know and tell them what I'm about to tell you."

When I got into the book of Galatians and the book of James where it discusses gossiping, I discovered God didn't like this little characteristic of mine. When someone would come into the office with a juicy little tid-bit, I couldn't wait until they left so I could tell someone else. I would say, "Do you know what I just heard?" Then, there I'd stand. The Holy Spirit would remind me that God didn't like gossiping, so during my first year as a Christian I spent half of my life with my mouth hanging wide open, much to the amazement of my friends who really thought I was nuts, but PRAISE JESUS, he taught me not to gossip.

That's YOUR RESPONSIBILITY! You can go ahead and be mean. You can go ahead and be bad-tempered and angry, or you can stop it, because God is doing his part constantly.

*For God is at work within you, helping
you want to obey him, and then helping
you do what he wants (Phil. 2:13).*

Remember, God will give you the
.... WANT
.... DESIRE
.... OPPORTUNITY and
.... POWER
but he leaves the final decision up to you. If you want to have the abundant life that Jesus promises, look at all the opportunities he gives you to do your part, and then DO THEM!

Now that we've learned what OUR part is, let's see what God promises when we do our part!

WHO AM I?

(by Frances)

(KJV except where stated)

One of the most exciting revelations you can ever have, is to discover who you really are in Christ! Many people are involved in "churchianity" and "church membership" which is not a personal relationship with Jesus Christ. What is the secret that makes one individual vibrant with the love of God shining through him, and another one completely defeated?

Paul is speaking:

> God has sent me to help his church and to tell his secret plan ... He has kept this secret for centuries and generations past, but now at last it has pleased him to tell it to those who love him and live for him, and the riches and glory of his plan are for you Gentiles, too. And this is the secret: that Christ in your hearts is your only hope of glory.
>
> So everywhere we go we talk about Christ to all who will listen, warning

> *them and teaching them as well as we*
> *know how. We want to be able to*
> *present each one to God, perfect because*
> *of what Christ has done for each of*
> *them. This is my work, and I can do it*
> *only because Christ's mighty energy is at*
> *work within me (Col. 1:25-29 TLB).*

CHRIST IN YOU, THE HOPE OF GLORY is the consistent theme throughout the Apostle Paul's writings. Paul is saying we cannot live the Christian life on our own. It is only because of Christ living IN us that we can! YOUR part is to find out who you are in Christ!

Christians who are defeated have not yet learned to stand upon the word and promises of God. Let's see what we have, as born-again believers, according to the word of God!

Ephesians 1:7   *In whom we have REDEMPTION*
                  through his blood, the FORGIVE-
                  NESS of sins, according to the
                  riches of his grace.

                  HALLELUJAH, I have REDEMP-
                  TION and FORGIVENESS OF
                  SINS!

Romans 5:1   *Therefore being justified by faith,*
                  we have PEACE WITH GOD
                  through our Lord Jesus Christ.

                  Glory! I have PEACE WITH GOD!
One of the most important things you can ever have is the ability to lay your head down on a pillow at

night, and go to sleep instantly because you have PEACE WITH GOD! There are people who would literally pay millions of dollars for peace of mind, and yet they never achieve it.

"In 1923 a very important meeting was held at the Edgewater Beach Hotel in Chicago. In attendance were nine of the world's most successful financiers. Those present were: the president of the largest independent steel company, the president of the largest utility company, the president of the largest gas company, the greatest wheat speculator, the president of the New York Stock Exchange, a member of the President's Cabinet, the greatest stock broker, the head of the world's greatest monopoly, the president of the Bank of International Settlements.

"Certainly we must admit that here was gathered a group of the world's most successful men; at least, men who had found the secret of making money. Twenty-five years later let's see where these men were:

> The president of the largest independent steel company, Charles Schwab, died bankrupt and lived on borrowed money for five years before his death. The president of the largest utility company, Samuel Insull, died a fugitive from justice and penniless in a foreign land. The president of the largest gas company, Howard Hopson, went insane. The greatest wheat speculator, Arthur Cotton, died abroad, insolvent. The president of the New York Stock Exchange, Richard Whitney, was released from Sing Sing Penitentiary. The member of the

President's Cabinet, Arthur Fall, was
pardoned from prison so he could die at
home. The greatest "bear" on Wall
Street, Jesse Livermore, died a suicide.
The head of the greatest monopoly, Ivan
Krueger, died a suicide. The president of
the Bank of International Settlements,
Leon Fraser, died a suicide. All of these
men learned well the art of making a
living, but not one learned how to live."

From Billy Rose, *Pitching Horse Shoes,* 1948. The
meeting at the Edgewater Beach Hotel was a youth
congress.

Praise God, in Jesus, we have learned how to live!

Romans 3:22   *Even the RIGHTEOUSNESS OF
                     GOD which is by faith of Jesus
                     Christ unto ALL and upon ALL
                     them that believe: for there is no
                     difference.*

Every morning when we wake up, we both say
something like, "Good morning, Jesus," or "Jesus, let
me love you more," but the second thing we say is,
"I'VE GOT THE RIGHTEOUSNESS OF GOD IN ME."
Try shouting that some morning from under the covers,
and see what it does for you! It can really start your
day off right, regardless of how you feel!

One time in Indiana we had just finished a crusade
and had gone to bed at midnight. At one o'clock in the
morning the devil took a real poke at me, and I came
down with a virus which was probably the most
devastating thing that has hit me in years. Hour by

hour, I got sicker and sicker, and weaker and weaker. By five o'clock in the morning, I told Charles I thought he and the Amigos (our singing group) would have to go to the next town without me. I said I'd come as soon as I was able.

By the time seven o'clock rolled around, I was so sick, I was almost hoping I would die! But I was too sick for Charles to leave me alone, so I said, "Don't leave me, honey. Carry me to the bus and I'll make it somehow!"

I didn't have enough strength to dress, so Charles borrowed a blanket and wrapped it around me. He half-carried me down the stairs and onto the bus. After the most miserable night of my entire life, I can imagine what I looked like! Amigo Chico was driving the bus, and I could tell his heart was breaking because of the way I felt. When I put my foot onto the bottom step of the bus to get on, I looked at him and said, "I'VE GOT THE RIGHTEOUSNESS OF GOD IN ME!" certainly didn't look it, I certainly didn't feel it, but I believed what the word of God says!

I laid down in one of the bedrooms, and the devil sure had a field day, because the air conditioner broke, and without it there is no ventilation on the bus. The temperature seemed to be about 120 degrees inside the bus! The more we drove, the sicker I got, but I kept saying, "I'VE GOT THE RIGHTEOUSNESS OF GOD IN ME!" When we arrived at our destination, Charles took me off, put me right to bed and he took the afternoon service alone. But do you know where I was at seven o'clock that evening? I WAS STANDING RIGHT WITH CHARLES AT A MIRACLE SERVICE! Hallelujah, I've got the righteousness of God in me! God hasn't lost a battle yet!

Say it right now, will you? I'VE GOT THE RIGHTEOUSNESS OF GOD IN ME! Say it tomorrow morning before you get out of bed and see what it does to you. God's part has already been done — he put his righteousness in you! Now your part is to believe it!

Col. 1:27   *Christ IN you, the hope of glory.*

Put your hand over your heart right now! Do you feel that heartbeat? That's the heartbeat of Jesus Christ living his life through you. When I first realized this, I put my hand over my heart, locked an imaginary door, and threw the key away, saying, "Jesus, I lock you in. Don't you ever get out of there!"

Praise God, I have Christ IN me! Say it!

Phil. 4:13   *I can do ALL things through Christ*
                     which strengtheneth me.

Do you have a problem over which you can't get victory?

Have you tried to quit smoking, only to return to vomit like a dog does?

Have you tried to quit drinking, only to sneak back again when no one is looking?

Have you tried to lose weight, but found yourself back in the kitchen at night gobbling down food over the sink, hoping that if no one caught you, it wouldn't count?

Lots of people think that verse says, "I can do all things except . . . ."

Your part is to appropriate that verse for yourself and your need! Say it right now. I CAN DO ALL

THINGS THROUGH CHRIST WHICH STRENGTHENETH ME!

I Cor. 2:16 *We have the MIND OF CHRIST!*

Did you ever think you weren't as smart as someone else? Did you ever let someone tell you that you were dumb? Don't ever feel that way again! Do you think Jesus was smart? I do, therefore we can't be stupid when we have the mind of Christ!

Say it: I HAVE THE MIND OF CHRIST! Doesn't that make you feel good? Especially if you say it REAL LOUD!

I Cor. 3:16 *Know ye not that ye are the TEMPLE OF GOD, and that the Spirit of God dwelleth in you?*

Praise Jesus, I am the TEMPLE OF GOD. I might not look like it to everyone, but God's word says it, so it's true!

I AM THE TEMPLE OF GOD! Glory!

Romans 8:1 *There is therefore now NO CON-DEMNATION to them which are in Christ Jesus, who walk not after the flesh, but after the Spirit.*

All my sins have been forgiven. I never have to feel guilty again about anything. Hallelujah! There is NO condemnation. A friend of mine who used to drink martinis with me said she felt guilty every time she passed a bar after she was saved. I said, "Not me! Every time I see some drunken woman, I praise God that he saved me from a fate like that." When God forgave me, my part was to accept his forgiveness. I did, and I couldn't take a drink today if someone offered me fifty million dollars!

What happened to the friend? She didn't stand on the word of God that there was now no condemnation, and she went back to drinking!

I HAVE NO CONDEMNATION because I am in Christ Jesus! Glory to God!

Romans 8:16   *The Spirit itself beareth witness with our spirit, that we are the CHILDREN OF GOD!*

Praise Jesus, I am a CHILD OF GOD!

Romans 8:2   *For the law of the Spirit of life in Christ Jesus hath made me FREE FROM THE LAW OF SIN AND DEATH.*

I AM FREE FROM THE LAW OF SIN AND DEATH! Glory!

Romans 8:17   *And if children, then heirs; HEIRS OF GOD, and JOINT-HEIRS WITH CHRIST.*

Father, I praise you, for giving me the privilege of being a JOINT-HEIR WITH JESUS!

Romans 8:28   *And we know that ALL THINGS
                 WORK TOGETHER FOR GOOD to
                 them that love God, to them who
                 are called according to his purpose.*

Sometimes we wonder why certain things happen. In the construction of our new operations building, the workers fell three months behind in its completion. We needed the space desperately, and couldn't understand why God allowed all the delays to happen. But we kept believing that ALL THINGS WORK TOGETHER FOR GOOD to them that love God. Suddenly we discovered the reason! Because of expansion that God knew about all along (but which we didn't know about) if the building had been completed on schedule, the interior would have been constructed wrong. By God allowing the delays, we discovered his expansion plans in time, and made the necessary changes!

                 Hallelujah, EVERYTHING works for
                 my good!

Romans 8:31   *If God be for us, who can be
                 against us?*

                 No one! GOD AND I ARE A
                 MAJORITY!

Romans 8:37   *WE ARE MORE THAN CON-
                 QUERORS through him that loved
                 us.*

                 I am a CONQUEROR, therefore I
                 cannot be defeated!

Romans 8:38,39   *For I am persuaded, that neither death, nor life, nor angels, nor principalities, nor powers, nor things present, nor things to come, Nor height, nor depth, nor any other creature, shall be able to separate us from the love of God, which is in Christ Jesus our Lord.*

NOTHING can separate me from the love of God!

Romans 10:8   *The word is nigh thee, even in thy mouth, and in thy heart: that is, the WORD OF FAITH, which we preach.*

I have the WORD OF FAITH in my mouth! Praise God!

Romans 6:23   *For the wages of sin is death; but the gift of God is ETERNAL LIFE through Jesus Christ our Lord.*

I have ETERNAL LIFE! What more can I ask?

Phil. 4:19   *But my God shall supply ALL YOUR NEED according to his riches in glory by Christ Jesus.*

ALL MY NEEDS SHALL BE MET!

I Peter 2:10
(TLB)

Once you were less than nothing;
NOW YOU ARE GOD'S OWN!

I'm somebody, because I BELONG
TO GOD!

Isaiah 62:3

Thou shalt also be a crown of glory
in the hand of the Lord, and a
royal diadem in the hand of thy
God.

One night when I opened my Bible, it fell open to
this chapter in Isaiah and I could hardly believe my
eyes to realize that I AM A CROWN OF GLORY and a
ROYAL DIADEM in the hand of the Lord! Glory!

2 Timothy 1:7

For God hath not given us the
spirit of fear; but of POWER, and
of LOVE, and of a SOUND MIND.

Did the devil ever try to tell you that you were
losing your mind, because you couldn't remember as
well as you used to? He tried that on me! But I stood
on the word of God and kept telling him that I had
POWER, LOVE and a SOUND MIND. Would you
believe I haven't forgotten a thing since then? (I write
everything down!) Fear is one of the most consuming
tricks of the devil these days, and this is a scripture we
ought to say over and over again.

I have POWER, LOVE and a SOUND MIND, so I
don't have to listen to the devil when he tries to get
my mind!

Can you stand some more of the fabulous promises of God? These will give you assurance of the fact that Christ lives within the heart of the believer. God has done his part — he put it in his word. Now your part is to believe it!

Revelation 3:20   *Behold, I stand at the door, and knock: if any man hear my voice, and open the door, I will come in to him, and will sup with him, and he with me.*

Hallelujah, JESUS IS IN MY HEART!

Hebrews 13:5   *He hath said, I WILL NEVER LEAVE thee, nor forsake thee.*

Glory to God, I'll NEVER BE ALONE AGAIN!

I John 1:9   *If we confess our sins, he is faithful and just to FORGIVE us our sins, and to CLEANSE us from all unrighteousness.*

I AM FORGIVEN; I AM CLEANSED!!

Romans 8:8-10   *So then they that are in the flesh cannot please God. But ye are not in the flesh, but IN THE SPIRIT, if so be that the SPIRIT OF GOD dwell IN YOU. Now if any man have not the Spirit of Christ, he is none of his. And if CHRIST be IN YOU, the body is dead because of sin; but the SPIRIT IS LIFE because of righteousness.*

I HAVE THE SPIRIT OF GOD IN ME, HALLELUJAH!

I Thess. 5:24   *Faithful is he that calleth you, who ALSO WILL DO IT.*

GOD WILL DO HIS PART; HE SAID SO!

Phil. 2:13   *For it is God which worketh IN you both to will and to do of his good pleasure.*

GOD WORKS IN ME!

Romans 5:10   *For if, when we were enemies, we were reconciled to God by the death of his Son; much more, being reconciled, we shall be SAVED by his life.*

HIS LIFE SAVES ME!

Gal. 2:20   *I am crucified with Christ: nevertheless I live; yet not I, but CHRIST LIVETH IN ME: and the life which I now live in the flesh I*

*live by the faith of the Son of God,
who loved me, and gave himself for
me.*

**AS IMPERFECT AS I AM, HE
LIVES IN ME!**

John 14:20,21   *At that day ye shall know that I
am in my Father, and YE IN ME,
and I IN YOU. He that hath my
commandments, and keepeth them,
he it is that loveth me: and he that
loveth me shall be loved of my
Father, and I will love him, and will
manifest myself to him.*

I AM IN HIM! HE IS IN ME!

I John 4:13,15,16 *Hereby know we that we dwell IN
him, and he IN us, because he hath
given us of his Spirit. Whosoever
shall confess that Jesus is the Son
of God, God dwelleth IN him, and
he IN God. And we have known
and believed the love that God hath
to us. God is love; and he that
dwelleth in love dwelleth in God,
and God in him.*

**I CONFESS THAT JESUS IS THE
SON OF GOD, THEREFORE GOD
DWELLS IN ME!**

I John 3:24   *And he that keepeth his commandments dwelleth in him, and he in him. And hereby we know that HE ABIDETH IN US, by the Spirit which he hath given us.*

I KNOW HE ABIDES IN ME!

John 7:38,39   *He that believeth on me, as the scripture hath said, out of his belly shall flow rivers of living water. (But this spake he of the Spirit, which they that BELIEVE ON HIM should RECEIVE: for the Holy Ghost was not yet given; because that Jesus was not yet glorified.)*

I BELIEVE!!! I RECEIVE!!!

As a daily prescription, how about saying the following every day:

I HAVE FORGIVENESS OF ALL MY SINS!
I HAVE PEACE WITH GOD!
I HAVE THE RIGHTEOUSNESS OF GOD IN ME!
I HAVE CHRIST IN ME!
I CAN DO ALL THINGS THROUGH CHRIST!
I HAVE THE MIND OF CHRIST!
I AM THE TEMPLE OF GOD!
I HAVE NO CONDEMNATION!
I AM A CHILD OF GOD!

I AM FREE FROM THE LAW OF
SIN AND DEATH!

I AM A JOINT-HEIR WITH
JESUS!

I KNOW THAT EVERYTHING
WORKS FOR MY GOOD!

GOD AND I ARE A MAJORITY!

I AM MORE THAN A CON-
QUEROR!

NOTHING CAN SEPARATE ME
FROM THE LOVE OF GOD!

I HAVE THE WORD OF FAITH
IN MY MOUTH!

I HAVE ETERNAL LIFE!

ALL MY NEEDS SHALL BE MET!

I AM SOMEBODY, BECAUSE I
BELONG TO GOD!

I AM A CROWN OF GLORY AND
A ROYAL DIADEM!

I HAVE POWER, LOVE AND A
SOUND MIND!

Col. 2:10 (TLB)

*So you have EVERYTHING when
you have Christ!* Hallelujah, I have
EVERYTHING.

Here's some additional good medicine to take daily:

JESUS IS IN MY HEART!

I'LL NEVER BE ALONE AGAIN!

I AM FORGIVEN; I AM
CLEANSED!

I HAVE THE SPIRIT OF GOD IN ME!

GOD WILL DO HIS PART!

GOD WORKS IN ME!

HIS LIFE SAVES ME!

HE LIVES IN ME!

I AM IN HIM; HE IS IN ME!

GOD DWELLS IN ME!

I KNOW HE ABIDES IN ME!

I BELIEVE. I RECEIVE!

Try these:

Eph. 1:3	I AM BLESSED!
John 16:24 (TLB)	MY CUP OF JOY IS OVERFLOWING!
I Peter 5:7 (TLB)	GOD IS ALWAYS THINKING ABOUT ME!
Psalm 37:23	MY STEPS ARE ORDERED BY GOD, Hallelujah!
Isaiah 26:3	I HAVE PERFECT PEACE, Hallelujah!
James 1:5	I HAVE WISDOM, Glory to God!
John 15:11 & I John 1:4	I HAVE JOY!
Isaiah 40:31	MY STRENGTH IS RENEWED!

Glory to God, even as I write these promises down, my soul is soaring up into the heavenlies. God has done his wonderful part in giving these promises. Our part is to find them and believe them!

LOOK FOR THE PROMISES!

THIS WAY UP!

GOD'S PROSPERITY IS FOR YOU

by Frances

God's PROSPERITY is for you!

God's prosperity is for YOU!

GOD'S prosperity is for you!

This one little sentence really says a lot!

The first time I ever made that statement, I put the emphasis on the word "prosperity." The second time I said it, I put the emphasis on the word "you." Then the third time I said it, I put the emphasis on the word "God!" Put them all together, and you have the answer to prosperity. When you put the emphasis on the word "God," however, it takes on an entirely different meaning, because in Psalm 50:10 it says my Father owns the cattle on a thousand hills.

GOD's prosperity is for you, and if he owns the cattle on a thousand hills, with the price of beef being what it is today, that means your Father is pretty wealthy, doesn't it?

Believe that God's prosperity is for you, and tap into the source which shows us that God's prosperity is truly for YOU! It's the same sentence, only this time the highlight is on YOU, because you're the one YOU are interested in. God's word says that God wants YOU to prosper! I used to think it was only preachers who talked about money. Then I became a Christian and read the word of God, and discovered that God says a tremendous amount about money in his Holy Word! The unique thing about it, however, is that God constantly talks about GIVING it away . . . and that's the secret. . . . GIVING IT AWAY!

Did YOU ever get a bad attitude when the preacher took up the offering? I did. I used to say, "Money, money, money, that's ALL they're interested in. That's the only reason they want me to come to church!" (And then I got saved. Hallelujah!)

Did you ever notice how uncomfortable many people get when someone begins to talk about an offering during a service? That's because they don't give enough!

What would happen if, at offering time, the speaker started off like this: "Will you all please open your wallets and purses right now because we're going to fill them up!" Can you imagine the mad rush to get to your wallet or your purse? Wouldn't that be sensational? I can just imagine everyone making a mad dash for the altar to be sure they got their share before it ran out!

Offering time IS blessing time!

How can that be? How can you be blessed when you're giving away money that you need yourself?

Let's see what God has to say about it!

III John 2 (KJV) says,

> *Beloved, I wish above all things that*
> *thou mayest prosper and be in health*
> *even as thy soul prospereth.*

Did you hear that? God says he wishes above ALL things, two things: that you may prosper and be in health.

He talks about prospering, and this means in every area of your life. He doesn't intend for you to just prosper in one area, but in every single area! It doesn't make any difference what area it is, AS LONG AS YOUR SOUL IS PROSPERING! Let your soul get fat, and every other area in your life will prosper, including your pocketbook!

God wants your MARRIAGE to prosper.

God wants your FAMILY relationships to prosper.

God wants your BUSINESS relationships to prosper.

God wants your CHURCH relationships to prosper.

God wants your relationships to your CHILDREN to prosper.

God wants your relationsips to your EMPLOYER to prosper.

God wants your HEALTH to prosper.

Did you ever have a time when things really looked bad, and you thought, "God doesn't love me. God has forgotten all about me. Here I am down here all by myself. He's not even thinking about me at all"?

God is thinking about you all the time, and in his wonderful, loving heart, he wants you to prosper at all times.

There isn't a single place in God's word where he says, "I want you to be sick and poor!" Did you know that? And if you want to know the secret, here it is!

Seven words in the sixth chapter of Luke, verse 38, really explain the secret of prosperity. If we didn't know anything else except these seven words, we could have the most abundant life in the world! It simply says,

For if you give, you will get.

Anyone can understand that simple statement, can't they? If you give, YOU WILL GET! That's a money-back guarantee signed by God!

Who's got to give?

YOU!

Who's going to get?

YOU!

It's as simple as that!

I found that out even before I was saved. I didn't realize that God's Holy Spirit had revealed to me one of the greatest truths in the Bible! I was in a hospital prior to an eye operation, and had read the first verse of the Twenty-third Psalm.

> I closed the Bible and began to pray, "Oh, God, don't let the operation hurt tomorrow. I can stand anything, but don't let it hurt when they operate on my eye." I did what we all do — I really ignored God during good times, and then ran screaming for help when the tide went against me!

> I tried to recall the words I had read: "The Lord is my shepherd; I shall not want." But I guess what I really did was to pick up my Bible again and look to see what it actually said. I think what I saw that night was the handwriting of God as he said, "Frances Gardner, (that was my name then) I LOVE YOU." Of all the people in the world, God told me he loved me.

> I think in one world-shattering moment I got a glimpse of what my life

had been — a constant, "Oh, God, YOU do this for me!" And never a thought as to what I COULD DO FOR HIM.

I didn't know what I was doing really, but in that moment I said, "God, I take back that prayer, and I don't care how much it hurts tomorrow, but I promise you this. When I get out of this hospital, I WILL SPEND THE REST OF MY LIFE SEEING WHAT I CAN DO FOR JESUS CHRIST, AND NOT WHAT HE CAN DO FOR ME." (From the book *God Is Fabulous* by Frances Hunter.)

Little did I realize that I was speaking the real answer to everything in the Christian life — GIVING!

The secret of living is giving! Do you see what I was doing? I was saying to God, "I'm willing to do everything I can for you. I don't ask you to do a thing for me. I just want to do everything I can for you."

Watch what God does when you're willing to do that! He says, "If you give, you will get." How will he give it back?

> *Your gift will return to you in full and overflowing measure, pressed down, shaken together to make room for more, and running over.*

Hallelujah!

That's not something that is a "maybe;" *maybe* God will return it that way. God's word says that IS the way he will return it to you. Your gift will return to you in full and overflowing measure, pressed down and shaken together to make room for more and running over. Glory!

If you give LOVE, you will get back LOVE!

If you give FELLOWSHIP, you will get back FELLOWSHIP!

If you give TIME to God, you will get back more TIME than you know what to do with!

If you give MONEY to God, you will get back MONEY!

Watch the next sentence, though, because this is where so many of us get trapped! It says

> *Whatever measure you use to give —*
> *large or small — will be used to measure*
> *what is given back to you.*

Did you know that according to the word of God, we actually are the ones who control the amount that God gives back to us? That's right. We really do, because God says he's going to use the same measure to give back to us that we use to give to him.

In the back of my Bible I have a tiny spoon. I often have a cup of tea on a plane, and the airlines give a little spoon to stir it with. It's the tiniest little spoon I have ever seen in my entire life! The bowl of the spoon at its longest part is a little over one-half inch. It is about one-sixteenth inch deep, and it's probably three-eights inch wide. Visualize in your mind what a tiny little spoon it is.

If I gave to God with that little spoon, God by his word is obligated to use that same little spoon to measure what he is going to give back to me. He'd take that tiny little spoon, and press it down, shake it together to make room for more, run it over, and then give it back to me. If you've ever seen one of those little spoons, or visualize it in your mind, you know how long it would take to move a big mountain with such a little spoon!

God can only work with what you give him!

Now I want you to think about something else. I want you to think about a big bushel basket. You can get a lot in a bushel basket. If you give to God with a great big bushel basket, just think how God can press it down, shake it together, and run it all over the place to give it back to you!

What's your part? Giving generously to God! If you do your part, God will do his part! Remember, you control what God can give to you by the measure you use to give to him.

GOD'S INTEREST RATE

Do you know what God's interest rate is? A lot of people don't. Listen to what Matthew 19:29 says

> *And anyone who gives up his home, brothers, sisters, father, mother, wife, children, or property, to follow me, shall receive a hundred times as much in return, and shall have eternal life.*

Did you hear that? That's a promise of God! You will receive a hundred times as much in return, plus the extra bonus of eternal life!

I believe the word of God is true! I have a feeling that YOU ALSO believe the word of God is true. It says, *"If you give you will get!"* Do you know a lot of people don't believe God? In our services, we always pray at every offering and ask God to multiply the gift back one hundredfold, Then we have a lot of fun reading letters people write telling us how God gave their money back. Many of them start off the same way:

"When you ministered here, I gave $2.00
in the offering. At that time you said it
would be multiplied a hundred times. I
TOOK THAT WITH A GRAIN OF
SALT and thought no more about it,
but just three months later a teacher
friend of mine who deals with her furni-
ture as a hobby came by, and after
seeing three pieces sitting on our front
porch said, 'I'll give you $200.00 for the
set.' Even then it didn't hit me, but later
I woke up to the realization there was
my $2.00 a hundred times over. Since I
believe God is fabulous just like you, I'm
wondering what he will do with this
$5.00 gift I'm sending you today."

The thing I want to bring out is that here is a
beautiful Christian woman, but she took the word of
God "with a grain of salt." Why do we do that? Why
don't we trust God?

When we BELIEVE that God is going to do what he
says he will, that is when we can live and walk and run
in prosperity!

Maybe you are thinking, "Well, that one was just
different. Everybody else is going to believe what you
say." No, they're not! The first letter was from Texas,
but this one from Nebraska is very interesting, too:

"Well, add me to your list. I have been a
born-again Christian for about three
years and have read and enjoyed most of
your books. When you were in Omaha, I
and my three children drove 100 miles
to be right there in the front row. I'm

afraid the devil was with us also, because while there was much happening that really moved me and certainly impressed my kids, ages 12, 10, and 7, there were also times when I was frankly skeptical. When the time came for the offering and Frances prayed that our gift would be returned one hundredfold, I became downright cynical. I thought that was a pretty effective pitch. I wrote out a check for $10.00 and said to myself, 'I can hardly wait to see how the Lord is going to come up with the thousand bucks,' knowing full well that there was no way that this could happen. Within two weeks I got a completely unexpected promotion, and the annual increase in my salary is well over $1,000.00. Praise the Lord!"

All I can add to that is a great big "Hallelujah! Thank you, Jesus!" because God does it all the time!

I wish you could be in our office and read the exciting letters we get from people who tell us how God returned their money.

Another lady says:

"At one of your meetings this summer I gave $20.00. Frances prayed that the gift would be multiplied a hundredfold. In September we were given $1,500.00 from a source we never dreamed of. I never connected the two incidents until I received the Hunter prayer letter this week. However, I wondered about the

other $500.00, since she had prayed for
a hundredfold and we had only received
$1,500.00. When I asked God, he re-
minded me that my son had received a
$500.00 scholarship to Oral Roberts Uni-
versity for this year. Praise God!"

Isn't it wonderful that even though God doesn't give it
to you all at one time, he does get around to giving the
entire thing to you?

Do you know what Charles and I do at offering time
in our church? We fold our check and put it between
Luke 6:38 and Matthew 19:29, and say, "God, we
expect you to act!"

There is a condition to that hundredfold promise of
God, however. Did you notice? It says if you are
willing to give up the things that you hold dear to you,
then God will return it to you a hundredfold! But we
have to meet God's conditions to make his promises
become a reality!

God wants you to prosper in exactly the same
manner that your soul is prospering. Your soul cannot
prosper until you are willing to do your part and give
God your entire life.

Someone once asked me, "What did it cost you to
get where you are today?" I simply replied, "Nothing,
except MY WHOLE LIFE!" That's all it takes, just
your entire life! The minute you are willing to say,
"God, I'll give you everything you want. I'll give you
first place in my life. I'll do anything you want," then
God will begin to move in the finances of your life.

But I want to tell you something else! You'd better
mean it when you say it, because God looks deep into
our hearts, and God knows exactly what our intentions
are and what we're thinking.

God knows whether we mean it or whether we don't. God knows if we're saying it but thinking, "I'll get to be a millionnaire this way." No, you won't. No, you won't! You won't get to be a millionnaire just thinking, "God is going to give me money." You've got to want to serve God with your mind, your heart, your body and your soul and to love him, and to be willing to do it even if you never had one dollar more than you have right now.

Do you want to know something exciting? The minute you are willing to say that, the minute you are willing to believe it, down in the deepest recesses of your soul, that's when God begins to open the windows of heaven and when God can really begin to move in your life!

But seek ye first the kingdom of God, and his righteousness; and all these things shall be added unto you (Matthew 6:33 KJV).

And the "things" he wants to add to you are "things" like happiness, health, prosperity, wisdom, knowledge and understanding. ALL of these "things" shall be added unto you. He didn't say some of them; he simply says ALL!

How God changes the spiritual into physical is always done in a very supernatural way. God expects us to do our part. I want you to clearly understand this, because I believe there have been too many Christians who have just sat down on a tree stump and said, "Well, God will provide my every need. God will provide my every need."

Yes, he will! But there is still that condition. It says to give him FIRST place in your life. Not second, not

third, not tenth, but FIRST place in your life. So if
you want financial prosperity, make your decision right
now that everything else takes second place to God!

If you give him first place, then you'll want to listen
to what he has to say about work, and God says a lot!
In this scripture, substitute employer and employee for
master and slave

> *Slaves, obey your masters; be eager to
> give them your very best. Serve them as
> you would Christ. Don't work hard only
> when your master is watching and then
> shirk when he isn't looking; work hard
> and with gladness all the time, as though
> working for Christ, doing the will of
> God with all your hearts. Remember, the
> Lord will pay you for each good thing
> you do, whether you are slave or free
> (Ephesians 6:5-8).*

I didn't become a Christian until I was 49 years of
age, and the first place God got me was in the
pocketbook. He said, "The devil has had your money
long enough. Now I want it. Give me twenty per cent
of everything you've got!" I was so excited because I
had finally discovered that God loved me as a person.
And it wouldn't have made any difference what he
asked me to do!

I was a brand new baby in Christ, someone who
didn't know what the word of God said, but someone
who felt the tremendous load of guilt lifted, and I
thought twenty per cent was God's charge for saving
me. It didn't make any difference to me! I was so
grateful to God for saving me that all I knew was I had
to be *obedient* to him. I listed everything I owned and
gave God twenty per cent!

I praise God for this, because in my complete and total ignorance of what the word of God promised, somehow or other, I knew enough to be obedient to the first thing he ever said to me.

I had never read the word of God!

I didn't know what it said.

I didn't know anything about the promises of God!

Do you know that doesn't make any difference? God has to fulfill his word when you have fulfilled the conditions of his word.

I was born again.

I said, "If you want what's left of this mess, take ALL of my life, not just part!"

I didn't know that God said he wanted me to prosper and be in health even as my soul prospered.

I didn't know this at all!

All I knew was that something had happened to me.

All I knew was that I had fallen in love with a man named Jesus!

All I knew was that God had reached down in a supernatural way and saved somebody who had lived in sin for forty-nine years. And in a beautiful, instant twinkling of an eye, God forgave every sin that I had ever committed. I didn't even know that salvation was free!

All I wanted to do was to love him and to obey him and to listen to him!

So I gave him twenty per cent of everything I had!

I didn't know for a long time what the word of God has to say about giving. I didn't know that Luke 6:38 said I was going to get back what I had given to God. But that didn't make any difference, because God began to fulfill his word and do you know what he did to me? He gave back to me. And how he shoveled it back on me was unbelievable!

He pressed it down!

He shook it together!

He let it run all over the place!

Do you know what I had to do then? I had to give it back to God. Do you know what God did when I gave back to him?

He gave back to me!

And I gave back to him,

and he gave back to me,

and I gave back to him,

and he gave back to me,

and I gave back to him,

and he gave back to me.

We've been having a running battle for years, and do you know what? I have not won the battle yet. I HAVE NEVER BEEN ABLE TO OUTGIVE GOD! (And I never will!) But I have never had a need in my life since the day I learned to give to God! Neither will you!

The secret of living is GIVING!

The word "give" is used in the Bible 816 times.

God has a lot to say about giving, doesn't he? How should you give? The Bible says *"Freely ye have received, freely give" (Matthew 10:8 KJV)*.

Did you notice that God always tells you to give generously? God never tells you to give in a stingy manner. He tells you to give liberally and generously. (Did the devil ever tell you that you couldn't afford to give? That's a lie, because there's no truth in him. He wants to rob you of God's blessings!) When you NEED a lot is when you can afford to give the most.

Freely you have received. Freely give.

> *He which soweth sparingly shall reap also sparingly; and he which soweth bountifully shall reap also bountifully (II Cor. 9:6 KJV).*

Think about a farmer sowing his crops. Some of us may never have been on a farm; some of us may have lived on a farm. Some of us may have even been born on a farm. But regardless of how much or how little we know about farming, I believe all of us understand the principle of raising food. If you want to get food out of the ground, you've got to put something in there first.

The farmer has to sow his seed. The farmer can't go out there and just pray and say, "God, send me a big crop." I can guarantee you if he does, he'll get nothing but a big crop of weeds. If he wants a bountiful crop, he must sow his seed bountifully.

He's going to get out there with a tractor and whatever farm equipment he has and make rows on his farmland. Then he's going to come along with a machine which is going to drop little seeds into the ground. If he's got three hundred acres that he wants to plant in wheat, he's not going to plant one little grain of wheat, is he? That one little grain of wheat is going to bring up more than itself, but if he really wants to get a good crop he is going to have to put a lot of seed in, isn't he?

Then he's going to have to take care of it! I don't think I ever knew a farmer who went out in the field and sowed three hundred acres with wheat and then just let it go and let the weeds grow up. Why? Because he wouldn't have a very good crop, would he?

No, he takes care of it! He puts fertilizer on it if the ground needs it. If there is no water available, he irrigates the land as they do out in west Texas. He gets in there and digs out the weeds and keeps the ground loose so the seeds will grow properly. The farmer has to work hard to see that his crop is going to be a bountiful one.

Exactly the same thing is true of a Christian. We've got to water and fertilize and keep the weeds out of our own personal life. If you want God's prosperity, get into the word of God, because it says *"So then faith cometh by hearing, and hearing by the word of God" (Romans 10:17 KJV)*. Get into the word of God and discover the promises God has for you!

When I first became a Christian, someone told me there were over 70,000 promises in the word of God! I said, "Wow! God, let me live long enough to claim them all!" That's why I've always been a fanatic for reading the Bible; I want to discover ALL the good things God has for me.

Those that sow bountifully shall reap bountifully. If you want your crop and your "God stock" to really prosper, I'd suggest you sow a lot!

As a matter of fact, this is the only way the word of God tells you that your money can be multiplied.

There is no other way!

It doesn't say, "Put it in a bank!"

It doesn't say, "Invest it in stocks and bonds!"

It doesn't say, "Do this or that."

It simply says, "GIVE!"

When you give, you set into action the heart of God, who can then supernaturally begin to give to you. I don't understand how God does it. I only know that he does it!

> *Every one must make up his own mind as to how much he should give. Don't force anyone to give more than he really wants to, for cheerful givers are the ones God prizes (II Cor. 9:7).*

When you give because you think you have to, and not because you want to, you are destroying the blessings of God for yourself. God loves a CHEERFUL giver!

Next Sunday morning when you are in church, after you have written out your check, hold that offering up in the air and say, "Oh, Lord Jesus, I thank you for this opportunity to give. I thank you for the souls this is going to save. I thank you for the person who is going to be healed as a result of this money. I thank you, dear Jesus, for the person who is going to receive the baptism with the Holy Spirit because of the way this money is going to be used. Thank you, Father, for that poor soul over in Africa who has never heard about Jesus, who is going to hear because some little bit of what I'm giving today will go all the way over there and lead someone to Jesus. Thank you, Father, for that dope addict in my own hometown that is going to reach out and be saved."

Now, if you want to get even closer, say, "Thank you, Lord Jesus, that this money is going to pay part of my pastor's salary, and that is why he can afford to stand up there today and work for you. Lord, thank you that a part of this is going to be responsible for the salvation of this person sitting right next to me today, the person that doesn't know Jesus."

Your heart is going to be cheerful when you give that way! You're going to get excited! Don't think about giving it away, but think how God is going to take that money and use it, then you'll be cheerful and excited! Your heart is going to be bubbling over with joy!

... And that's the way God wants you to give!

> *If you are really eager to give, then it isn't important how much you have to give. God wants you to give what you have, not what you haven't (II Cor. 8:12).*

If you are really eager to give, then he is going to bless you all over the place! He wants you to EAGERLY give to him. Did you notice the little warning tagged on to the end of that scripture? NO HOT CHECKS!

> *God is able to make it up to you by giving you everything you need and more, so that there will not only be enough for your own needs, but plenty left over to give joyfully to others.*

Another promise — all your needs will be met, and plenty left over!

> *It is as the Scriptures say: "The godly man gives generously to the poor. His good deeds will be an honor to him forever." For God, who gives seed to the farmer to plant, and later on, good crops to harvest and eat, will give you MORE and MORE seed to plant and will make it grow so that you can give away more and more fruit from your harvest.*

How much plainer can God get? Once you start the "return" system to God, he will give back more and more to you. Hallelujah!

> *Yes, God will give you much so that you can give away much, and when we take your gifts to those who need them they will break out into thanksgiving and praise to God for your help. So, two good things happen as a result of your gifts — those in need are helped, and they overflow with thanks to God. Those you help will be glad not only because of your generous gifts to themselves and to others, but they will praise God for this proof that your deeds are as good as your doctrine (II Cor. 9:8-13).*

Why is God going to give you much? So that you can continue to give it away, so he can continue to give it back to you and bless you!

ALL MY NEEDS?

> *But my God shall supply ALL your need according to his riches in glory by Christ Jesus (Phil. 4:19 KJV).*

Hallelujah, God is going to supply ALL my need, not just some of them, but ALL of them! Many times we think God is going to supply all of our needs according to OUR riches, and that's why we depend upon our own money instead of depending upon God. But he promises according to HIS riches!

Do you remember the story of the rich young ruler? He asked Jesus what he had to do to have eternal life. He told Jesus that he had kept all the commandments from the time he was a young man. So Jesus told him to sell what he had and GIVE the money to the poor. (See the 18th chapter of Luke.)

Here is a young man who obviously was very intelligent, a young man who was very rich, a young man who had protected a fortune. I assume that as a rich young ruler he probably inherited a great amount of money, but I know people who have inherited a lot of money and have promptly gone out and blown it, don't you?

Think about the prodigal son in Luke 15. He wanted his share, so he took it and immediately went out and squandered it in riotious living. But the rich young ruler was a very intelligent man. He had guarded safely what he had. God knew this! He knew that he could trust this rich young ruler with much, so he wanted to give him a lot more.

In order to fulfill what the word says, the young man had to first GIVE away what he had, so God could multiply it back to him one hundredfold. God wanted to give that rich young ruler a tremendous empire. But unfortunately, he loved his money more than anything else!

Isn't it pathetic that he didn't know that God was going to give it back to him one hundredfold? He went sadly away, and nowhere in the word of God does it mention that the rich young ruler was ever saved.

He lost two things: he lost the most important thing of all, because he lost eternal life.

Second, he lost the riches God wanted to give him. But, do you know what I believe Jesus really wanted for him? There are certain words in the Bible that are used over and over again for the same purpose. Whenever Jesus said, *"Come, follow me,"* you will notice he called a disciple.

When Jesus was talking to the man he said, *"Sell all you have and give the money to the poor — it will become treasure for you in heaven — and come, follow me (Luke 18:22).*

The three words that he spoke to Andrew, Peter, James and John were, *"Come, follow me."* He said the same thing to the rich young ruler. But because he loved his money, he turned his back on everything. Doesn't your heart really cry for him, when you think about all he gave up — for what? For selfishness! The same thing can happen when Christians tighten up their pocketbooks and stop giving to God!

> *Lay not up for yourselves treasures upon earth, where moth and rust doth corrupt, and where thieves break through and steal: But lay up for yourselves treasures in heaven, where neither moth nor rust doth corrupt, and where thieves do not break through nor steal: For where your treasure is, there will your heart be also (Matt. 6:19-21 KJV).*

For a long time I thought this scripture said, "Where your heart is, there will your treasure be also." I thought it meant that if your heart was in heaven, then you would automatically give to God, but it says just the opposite! It says, *"Where your treasure is, there will your heart be also."* Start putting your money in the things of this world (and there are many things that are designed to make us feel we have to have them to live), and you'll discover that's where your heart will also be. Did you ever notice someone who had an uncontrollable desire to buy a new car? And usually a car that is off-limits because of the price? Their interest will be in showing off the new car, and not in the things of God!

I'm thinking of a young man who lives in Florida and owns a boat. A lot of his money is tied up in the boat, because a boat is an expensive thing to have. That's where his heart is, so what happens? He doesn't want to go to church on Sunday, because his heart is in that boat! Why is his heart in that boat? Because that's where his money is. He thinks his treasure is being lost if the boat just sits there and he doesn't get to go out on it.

If you want to walk the abundant Christian life and you want to have ALL the good things God has for you, put your treasure in heaven. Then, where your treasure is, is where your heart is going to be, because you're going to want to protect that treasure.

It's very interesting what happened between the Old Testament and the New Testament. In the Old Testament, God made a covenant with the people. We all know what the Bible has to say about tithing.

> *Bring ye all the tithes into the store-house, that there may be meat in mine house, and prove me now herewith, saith the Lord of hosts, if I will not open you the windows of heaven, and pour you out a blessing, that there shall not be room enough to receive it (Malachi 3:10 KJV).*

In the Old Testament, God gave first. To the people of Israel he gave first. He gave them good land; he gave them good crops. He gave them everything they needed.

God gave first, and he asked only one thing in return. He said, "You give me back ten per cent." God made an interesting discovery. Do you know what it was? God discovered that the human race cannot be trusted, because God gave generously, bountifully, extravagantly to the Israelites and found out they couldn't be trusted. Why? Because they did not bring their ten per cent back into the storehouse.

He did his part, but they didn't do their part.

Then came the New Testament, and God gave a new covenant. God knows that he can be trusted. That's why in the New Testament he says, "You give first, and then I'll give back to you, pressed down, shaken together, and running all over the place."

See the difference between the Old Testament and the New Testament? In the Old Testament, God gave first. In the New Testament he says, "YOU give first. You can always trust me, even though I can't always trust you!"

Look at the beautiful promise God gave to the people of Israel in Malachi 3:10.

> *If I will not open you the windows of heaven, and pour you out a blessing, that there shall not be room enough to receive it (KJV).*

How could anybody not give to God when he promises to return it that way! If God says it, I believe it!

MY MOUTH IS FULL OF MONEY

How do we really stand upon the word of God? There's another beautiful promise in Mark, but we have to confess with our mouths that we BELIEVE God is going to do what he says he is going to do. Living in God's prosperity and appropriating God's prosperity is so very simple, because it's just a question of believing God and then appropriating that power.

Mark 11:23,24 (KJV) says:

> *For verily I say unto you, That whoso-*
> *ever shall say unto this mountain, Be*
> *thou removed, and be thou cast into the*
> *sea; and shall not doubt in his heart, but*
> *shall believe that those things which he*
> *saith shall come to pass; he shall have*
> *whatsoever he saith.*

HE SHALL HAVE WHATSOEVER HE SAITH!!!

Now for the 24th verse

> *Therefore, I say unto you, What things*
> *soever ye desire, when ye pray, BE-*
> *LIEVE that ye receive them, and ye*
> *shall have them (KJV).*

Does that say, "Maybe you are going to get; maybe you are not?"

Does it say you have a fifty-fifty chance, or does it say you ARE going to receive?

It says IF you believe when you pray, you're going to receive!

There is another condition in the first part of verse 23. It says, *"and shall not doubt in his heart."*

Can you really trust God?

Can you really believe the word of God?

Can you really believe and stand on it with your heart, your mind, your body and your soul, that God will do what he says he will?

Of course you can!

God's word says that God cannot lie (see Titus 1:2 and Hebrews 6:18), and I believe this. The Almighty God who created this universe CANNOT lie (Num. 23:19).

When it says *"whosoever"* shall say it, that means YOU, and that means ME!

Is one of your desires to really be financially prosperous? There isn't anything wrong with that! The word of God says the *"LOVE of money is the root of all evil"* (I Timothy 6:10) but it certainly doesn't say that money is evil, because if it were evil, God certainly would not say that he wanted you to prosper. God has no desire for you to have anything evil!

Psalm 84:11 (KJV) says

> *No good thing will be withhold from them that walk uprightly.*

Do we really walk uprightly?

Do we really love Jesus?

Do we really believe God?

If so, he's not going to withhold a single good thing from us!

Psalm 42:11 says, *"Expect God to act."* If we really expect God to act in our finances, he will. When we begin confessing with our mouth that we expect God to act in the finances of our life, he will!

I want you to say something with me right now. I want you to claim this promise of God, and then expect God to act. If you have a financial need in your life, put the amount you need in this prayer:

> Lord Jesus, I'm going to say with my mouth and with no doubt in my heart, I need a financial miracle of $_____. Thank you for this miracle.

Put in the figure that you need. I don't care if you need fifty dollars. I don't care if you need five thousand dollars. I don't care if you need a half-million dollars. I don't care if you need five million dollars. Put your need down! (I didn't say your financial DESIRES, because they can sometimes get out of line!) Ask God for whatever you need right now, and believe that God is going to do it.

Suppose right now that $10,000.00 would be the answer to your problem in life. I want you to believe God right now for $10,000.00. The Bible says if you believe and don't doubt in your heart, but believe that those things which you say shall come to pass, you SHALL HAVE WHATSOEVER YOU SAY!

Right now I want you to say with me, "God, I thank you for the way you will provide it. I thank you, God, because the way you provide it will be supernatural. I thank you, God, because you are who you are, and your word does not lie. I thank you, Father, for the way you're answering my prayer."

If you prayed that prayer, you SAID it, and if you believe it, and if there is no doubt in your heart, then it shall come to pass exactly the way God says! There's money in your mouth!

Here's a good four-fold plan for praying for your financial needs. God gives us a powerful formula for effective praying. We call it Formula Four, and we hope you will follow it, because we believe you will find your prayer life more rich and meaningful.

FORMULA FOUR

Here is Formula Four as recorded in Philippians 4:6:

No. 1 — *Don't worry about anything.*

> There is a vast difference between worry and concern. God's word tells us not to worry.

That's made possible by the second step of the formula.

No. 2 — *Pray about everything.*

Nothing is too small or too big for God. If your problem is big enough to concern you, it is big enough to take to God in prayer.

No. 3 — *Tell God your needs.*

Provision for our needs is a promise to the believer. God wishes you to share your needs with him, and he will provide.

No. 4 — *Don't forget to thank him for his answers.*

A grateful heart spilling over with praise is necessary for effective praying.

Formula Four works! Try it every day. You will find your prayer life and your needs, plus your financial prosperity, becoming a beautiful relationship of communication between you and Jesus!

Here's what the Living Bible says after you have fulfilled those first four things:

> *If you do this you will experience God's peace, which is far more wonderful than the human mind can understand. His peace will keep your thoughts and your hearts quiet and at rest as you trust in Christ Jesus. And now, brothers, as I close this letter let me say this one more*

> *thing: Fix your thoughts on what is true*
> *and good and right. Think about things*
> *that are pure and lovely, and dwell on*
> *the fine, good things in others. Think*
> *about all you can praise God for and be*
> *glad about (Philippians 4:7,8).*

What's your part?	What's God's part?
Giving!	Giving more back to you than you give!
Expecting God to act!	Acting!
Walking uprightly!	Not withholding anything good from you!
Saying and believing!	Giving you what you say and believe!
Laying up treasures in heaven!	Supplying all your needs!
Giving cheerfully!	Giving you more and more so you can give away more!
Sowing generously.	Giving you enough to reap bountifully!
Seeking the kingdom of God and his righteousness first!	Adding all these things unto you!

Giving up everything!   Giving it back to you one
                          hundredfold!

PROSPERITY PROMISES FOR YOU
(Say these daily and see what happens!)

Blessed is the man that walketh not in the counsel of the ungodly, nor standeth in the way of sinners, nor sitteth in the seat of the scornful. But his delight is in the law of the Lord; and in his law doth he meditate day and night. And he shall be like a tree planted by the rivers of water, that bringeth forth his fruit in his season; his leaf also shall not wither; and WHAT-SOEVER HE DOETH SHALL PROSPER! (Psalm 1:1-3 KJV).

EVERYTHING I DO SHALL PROSPER, thank you Lord!

The young lions do lack, and suffer hunger: but they that seek the Lord SHALL NOT WANT ANY GOOD THING (Psalm 34:10 KJV).

I SHALL NOT WANT FOR ANY GOOD THING!

I love them that love me; and those that seek me early shall find me. Riches and honour are with me; yea, durable riches and righteousness. My fruit is better than gold, yea, than fine gold; and my revenue than choice silver. I lead in the way of righteousness, in the midst of the paths of judgment: That I may cause those that love me TO INHERIT SUBSTANCE; AND I WILL FILL THEIR TREASURES (Proverbs 8:17-21 KJV).

HALLELUJAH, GOD IS GOING TO FILL MY TREASURES!

Look these up and see what they say to you:

Proverbs 10:22 (I AM BLESSED)

Proverbs 11:24,25 (TLB) (THE MORE I GIVE AWAY, THE RICHER I BECOME!)

Proverbs 11:28 (Check this in both KJV and TLB) I'M FLOURISHING!

Proverbs 14:11 (PRAISE GOD, MY HOUSE SHALL FLOURISH!)

Proverbs 19:23 (I'M ABIDING SATISFIED)

Proverbs 22:4 (HALLELUJAH, riches, and honour and life are MINE!)

If you can trust God with your soul, you can trust him with your money!

THIS WAY UP TO FINANCIAL PROSPERITY!

QUIT SINNING

(by Charles)

Frances' favorite sermon has two little words, that's all! QUIT SINNING!

God plainly told Jeremiah,

> *But if you STOP YOUR SINNING and begin obeying the Lord your God, he will cancel all the punishment he has announced against you (Jer. 26:13).*

That is still God's message for any who live today — QUIT SINNING!

Most problems can be solved simply if we do that one thing — stop sinning! God will even this day cancel all the punishment he has announced against us, and our problems will vanish, canceled by God.

> *Get some sense and quit your sinning (I Cor. 15:34).*

The King James Version doesn't express it quite as exciting, but it says, *"Awake to righteousness, and sin not."* In other words, when you awaken to the fact that you have the righteousness of God in you, you'll quit sinning! God has warnings about sinning throughout the Bible. And yet, all through history,

people have ignored his warnings and have kept on
sinning. No wonder they keep having problems! It's
hard to live in opposition to God's laws. It's like rowing
against the wind.

OUR PART: Quit Sinning.

GOD'S PART: To give us the power, which he does
through the Holy Spirit!

How do we stop sinning?

Quit!

It's that simple.

That's right, it's that simple!

A woman came to Frances one night with a very sad
story. She started off by saying, "I've been prayed for
by the best, so I don't know why I'm coming to you,
but . . .

I've had the demon of smoke cast out!

I've had the demon of tobacco cast out!

I've had the demon of nicotine cast out!

I've had the demon of cigarettes cast out!" She
continued, "Do you have a word from the Lord for
me?"

Frances said, "Yes!"

"What is it?" she asked.

Frances said, "Quit!"

The woman was obviously shocked. But too many
times we blame spirits or demons for things that are
simply our fault. We run from evangelist to evangelist,
from preacher to preacher, from conference to conference, asking for deliverance at every service, when
the problem is really very simple. It lies within ourself
– QUIT SINNING! Throw those cigarettes away, and
don't buy any more!

If, with all your heart, mind, body and soul, you
want to be obedient to all that God and Jesus want

you to do, there will never be a desire to sin. A desire to sin is simply a way of expressing your disbelief that God's way is best. God doesn't like that. But it delights him when you want to do what pleases him!

> *Learn as you go along what pleases the Lord. Take no part in the worthless pleasures of evil and darkness, but instead, rebuke and expose them (Eph. 5:10).*

Who must learn what pleases the Lord?
We must!
Who must rebuke and expose the pleasures of evil?
We must!

God's part is to tell us what sin is, and to make us aware of right and wrong. After he does his part, then it's up to us to quit sinning and obey him.

The fifth chapter of Galatians gets real specific in the sins so many "Christians" want to commit. God's part is stated in verse 16.

> *I advise you to obey only the Holy Spirit's instructions. He will tell you where to go and what to do, and then you won't always be doing the wrong things your evil nature wants you to.*

That's God's part.

The Holy Spirit guides us. He will always do his part, but he never forces us to obey God.

This same chapter states very plainly in verse 21, 22 the results of either following after the Holy Spirit, or following after our own natural desires.

> *Anyone living that sort of life will not inherit the kingdom of God. But when the Holy Spirit controls our lives he will*

> *produce this kind of fruit in us: love,*
> *joy, peace, patience, kindness, goodness,*
> *faithfulness, gentleness and self-control.*

What is our part? QUIT SINNING! As long as we sin, there's going to be guilt in our heart. When we have guilt, we can't have joy and peace, can we? And yet that's what the Bible promises if the Holy Spirit controls us. If the Holy Spirit controls us, we won't want to sin, will we?

Our minds are drawn over and over again to that beautiful promise of God in Philippians 2:13.

> *For God is at work within you, helping*
> *you want to obey him, and then helping*
> *you do what he wants.*

God wants the WANT into our hearts to please him by obeying him. He only tells us to do what he knows is good for us ... and then he helps us do what he wants us to.

What is sin?

Sin is our willful disobedience of God's laws.

Who sins?

God doesn't.

Jesus doesn't.

Then it is only we who sin, and we do it willingly and deliberately.

Why?

To please self instead of God.

We believe every person who is a Christian — and a lot who are not — want to quit sinning. What is the problem, then? Is it that we don't recognize the sin we are committing?

No, because then it wouldn't be a sin.

Is it because we don't want to face facts?

Could be!

Is it because we are not honest with ourselves and God?

Could be!

Whose part is it to face facts and be honest?

It's OUR part, always.

In order to sin, you have to WANT to sin. That's a horrible thought, isn't it? But it's true. Sin is our willful transgression of God's law. Sinning, when we do it, is totally and completely OUR PART. God has nothing to do with it.

But how do I quit?

Pray with us right now:

> Father, I know I have let sins be hidden in the darkness of my mind, just because I wanted to hide them from you. I'm sorry. Forgive me. Please open my mind and heart to want and desire what pleases you and Jesus. Remind me everytime I choose to please myself, rather than you. When you do your part in reminding me and showing me my sins, I will do my part and quit sinning. I will do it because I WANT TO! Your plan to have me in your family by sending Jesus to die for me was done by you BECAUSE YOU WANTED TO! Jesus died for me because he wanted to obey you. Father, I want to obey you, too. I promise, in the mighty name of Jesus.

Now, let's learn how to recognize the voice of the Holy Spirit when he reminds us of our sins.

Remember, all sins start with thoughts.

> *And then he added, "It is the thought-life that pollutes. For from within, out of men's hearts, come evil thoughts of lust, theft, murder, adultery, wanting what belongs to others, wickedness, deceit, lewdness, envy, slander, pride, and all other folly. All these vile things come from within; they are what pollute you and make you unfit for God" (Mark 7:20-23).*

We have to do our part in letting these thoughts be right thoughts. When we sense an approaching thought that is not going to please God, the Spirit will let us know even before it becomes a part of our mind's understanding. We call this a "piece" of a thought.

Learn to be so sensitive to following after the Holy Spirit that you will recognize an approaching thought.

If it's a good thought,

. . . receive it,

. . . accept it.

If it is an evil or unsatisfactory thought,

. . . reject it.

. . . Don't let it into your mind.

. . . Quit thinking about it.

. . . Quit sinning!

Once it has entered into your conscious mind, it becomes a part of your mind. It is recorded into your mind. Quickly change your thought pattern. Deliberately put another thought you know is right into your mind. Do your part; change your thinking quickly, so you don't give a foothold to the devil. He wants your mind, but God wants it more.

James 1:15 says *"Evil thoughts lead to evil actions and afterwards to the death penalty of God."*

When you reject an evil thought, it leaves your mind clean, but empty. The best filler for your mind is the word of God. Learn some good verses from the Bible so you can quickly replace approaching thoughts with verses you say with your mouth. When you say a verse, or think it, it becomes a part of your mind. It is a filler for your mind. It becomes a part of you that you can keep forever! It leads you to have a portion of the very mind of Christ.

Here are some good thought-stoppers; some mind-fillers for you to memorize. Quickly recall them to become a shield from the darts of Satan — which he sends directly to attack your mind.

> *I beseech you therefore, brethren, by the mercies of God, that ye present your bodies a living sacrifice, holy, acceptable unto God, which is your reasonable service (Rom. 12:1 KJV).*

Whose part is that?

Our part.

We are to present our bodies to God holy and acceptable.

How?

By sacrificing our own desires and replacing them with his desires.

> *There is therefore now no condemnation to them which are in Christ Jesus, who walk not after the flesh, but after the Spirit (Romans 8:1 KJV).*

If you slip and let the devil get an unwelcome thought into your mind, you don't have to feel guilty and condemned. Just tell God that you are sorry, and then push that thought away by saying with your mouth the above scripture that says you have no condemnation from God, because you don't want to walk after the flesh and think about things you want to do to please yourself. God has already said it, now it's your part to say and do it!

> *For I am not ashamed of the gospel of Christ: for it is the power of God unto salvation to every one that believeth (Romans 1:16 KJV).*

It is important that we tell others about the Good News that Jesus saves!

> *For if you tell others with your own mouth that Jesus Christ is your Lord, and believe in your own heart that God has raised him from the dead, you will be saved. For it is by believing in his heart that a man becomes right with God; and with his mouth he tells others of his faith, confirming his salvation (Romans 10:9,10).*

Whose part is it to tell?
Our part.
What is God's part?
He confirms our salvation.
Hallelujah!
Frances often tells how God cleaned up her mind when he saved her, and that a dirty joke has never entered her mind since! One day she said, "I don't think I could remember a dirty joke if my life depended on it!" Quickly I said, "Don't try!"

Certainly you can recall things that have been stored in your mind long ago, even in sinful days. But you don't have to! YOU stop sinning! Stop the thoughts

before you try to recall them. Don't repeat dirty jokes
and other unwanted things you hear during the day to
your wife, husband or friend. Don't let them become a
part of your conscious mind. That's a part you can
easily do.

Don't repeat gossip! God will not force us to stop
anything that we want to do or think, but he will
remind us, if we want him to. He always does his part
when we want to do ours.

One of the most frequently requested prayers is from
people who say, "Ask God to get these lustful thoughts
out of my mind." That's not a proper prayer.

That's not God's part; that's OUR part!

> *No one lights a lamp and hides it!*
> *Instead, he puts it on a lampstand to*
> *give light to all who enter the room.*
> *Your eyes light up your inward being. A*
> *pure eye lets sunshine into your soul. A*
> *LUSTFUL EYE SHUTS OUT THE*
> *LIGHT AND PLUNGES YOU INTO*
> *DARKNESS. So watch out that the sun-*
> *shine isn't blotted out. If you are filled*
> *with light within, with no dark corners,*
> *then your face will be radiant too, as*
> *though a floodlight is beamed upon you*
> *(Luke 11:33-35).*

Who opens or shuts a lustful eye? WE DO. God doesn't.
But he will remind us to "watch out" when a lust scene
first comes before our eyes.

What are some kinds of lust the Bible warns us to
reject? Read, memorize or learn to recognize them:

. . . lust for money (Job 22:24)
. . . lust for gain (Ezek. 28:18)
. . . lust for evil things (Ps. 141:4)
. . . lust for beauty (Prov. 6:25);

Look in your concordance to find other hidden lust
that the devil deceives you with to make you think you
are not guilty. Look how severe God deals with lust for
a girl.

> *I made a covenant with my eyes not to
> look with lust upon a girl. I know full
> well that Almighty God above sends
> calamity on those who do. He sees
> everything I do, and every step I take
> (Job 31:1-4).*

You can't help seeing girls in front of your eyes as they
come into your peripheral view. But you can keep from
taking a second peek if they have a lustful look. And
you can keep from thinking about it to stop lust from
coming into your conscious mind, and you can keep
from telling it to others. That's OUR part! The same is
true about any lust, anything we desire that puts God
in second place.

> *If I have put my trust in money, if my
> happiness depends on wealth, or if I
> have looked at the sun shining in the
> skies, or the moon walking down her
> silver pathway, and my heart has been
> secretly enticed, and I have worshiped
> them by kissing my hand to them, this,
> too, must be punished by the judges.
> For if I had done such things, it would
> mean that I denied the God of heaven
> (Job 31:24-28).*

Our part is to be very careful of what we want. We
must be very sure in every thought and desire that it is
what God wants, and not something to please self.
When we do ALL we can to please God, he will always

bring the greatest pleasures to us. The deceitful pleasures Satan offers are as eternally destructive to us as they were to Eve. His pleasures only make us want more; they never really satisfy. They temporarily seem to, and that's all!

Read Galatians and Ephesians to detect sins in your life which have been hidden in the darkness. Open your mind to God to let his light beam upon them. Then admit to yourself and to God that you have entertained those unwelcomed guests.

When you have done your part in keeping the darkness of sin out of your heart and mind, when you QUIT SINNING, then God has freedom to do HIS part.

> *Then it will be as though I had sprinkled clean water on you, for you will be clean — your filthiness will be washed away, your idol worship gone. And I will give you a new heart — I will give you new and right desires — and put a new spirit within you. I will take out your stony hearts of sin and give you new hearts of love. And I will put my Spirit within you so that you will obey my laws and do whatever I command (Ezek. 36:25-27).*

OUR MOTTO: *WHEN IN DOUBT, THROW IT OUT!*

GOD'S PART — TO GIVE AN ABUNDANT LIFE!

OUR PART — TO LIVE AN ABUNDANT LIFE!

Glory!

THIS WAY UP!

DO IT!

(OBEDIENCE)

(By Charles)

Can I attain perfect obedience, and still enjoy life?
   That's the only way!
   OUR PART: Obey God.
   GOD'S PART: He will give you everything you need
for living a truly good life!

> *Do you want more and more of God's
> kindness and peace? Then learn to know
> him better and better. For as you know
> him better, he will give you, through his
> great power, everything you need for
> living a truly good life (2 Peter 1:2,3).*
>
> *Next, learn to put aside your own
> desires so that you will become patient
> and godly, gladly letting God have his
> way with you (2 Peter 1:6).*
>
> *Tell me where you want me to go and
> I will go there (Ps. 86:11).*

Jesus' mother, Mary, replied to the angel,

> *I am the Lord's servant, and I am willing*
> *to do whatever he wants (Luke 1:38).*

Notice which of the above promises are our part:

. . . learn to know God better.

. . . learn to put aside your own desires.

. . . be willing to go wherever God wants you to go.

. . . be willing to do whatever God wants you to do.

After years of working my heart out in church, I finally spoke to God from the depths of my heart and said, "God, take ALL of my life and make me spiritually what you want me to be." It was at that moment I no longer had to obey (legalistically) what the Bible said. From that time on, all I wanted to do was to obey my God. My life changed from one of struggle to one of complete abundance. With all his heart God wants us to obey him with all our heart, with our every desire and thought.

> *If you will only help me to want your*
> *will, then I will follow your laws even*
> *more closely. Just tell me what to do*
> *and I will do it, Lord. As long as I live*
> *I'll wholeheartedly obey (Ps. 119:32-34).*

Think of all the sacrifices God required of the Old Testament children of Israel! Think of the efforts they made to obey God's laws to the very letter. But God said through Samuel to King Saul,

> *Obedience is far better than sacrifice. He*
> *is much more interested in your listening*
> *to him than in your offering the fat of*
> *rams to him (I Sam. 15:22).*

About four months after I totally commited my life, without reservation, to serve God, he gave me the first instructions I can remember. He said, "Go into my word and listen to no man and let me tell you what I want you to know." My immediate response was to pick up my Bible and say, "Yes, Father." I obeyed by meditating more than 2,000 hours in the New Testament the first year. Never had I been so close to God and to Jesus! Never had they spoken into my heart and mind so many promises and corrections. How I wanted to obey their laws!

I found complete peace in total surrender to the laws of God which he wrote on my heart as he revealed Jesus and his desires to me. No thrill is like the thrill of knowing you have obeyed the very wishes of the Almighty God! Never had I known such security! Never had I known love like the love of God that poured into me as I yielded my every thought to him in obedience to the call he was placing on my life! Oh, the glory of it!

Abundance? I never even dreamed there was such a wonderful, thrilling, exciting life full of abundance that God gave in response to my complete obedience to his desires, to his will and ways. My part was to give ALL to God, and, oh, how well he did his part, abundantly more than I could ever hope or dream!

It is when the law becomes a law of our heart, a desire, a longing to do all that pleases God, that we can really know God's heart.

> *For by that one offering he made forever perfect in the sight of God all those whom he is making holy. And the Holy Spirit testifies that this is so, for he has said, "This is the agreement I will make with the people of Israel, though they*

> *broke their first agreement: I will write*
> *my laws into their minds so that they*
> *will always know my will, and I will put*
> *my laws in their hearts so that they will*
> *want to obey them (Heb. 10:14-16. See*
> *also Hebrews 8:10).*

No longer was there a reluctance to tithe my income to God. I wanted to give and give and give! God had truly written a law of unselfishness in my heart and I wanted to obey his every wish.

No longer did I struggle to read God's word. I wanted to read it and to meditate on it day and night!

No longer did time close me into a forty or fifty hour work-week. My time ALL belonged to God. My weeks grew into more than one hundred hours of service to him.

When we have ministered long hours and the time is late at night, even when we are exhausted, there is that constraining love of Jesus within us that wants to minister to one more who has a need. The magnet of love that pulls our hearts to the heart of God is the most powerful pull known to mankind! My heart means it as much as did the totally surrendered heart of Paul when he said,

> *For I am persuaded, that neither death,*
> *nor life, nor angels, nor principalities,*
> *nor powers, nor things present, nor*
> *things to come, Nor height, nor depth,*
> *nor any other creature, shall be able to*
> *separate us from the love of God, which*
> *is in Christ Jesus our Lord (Romans*
> *8:38,39 KJV).*

I think of the time I meditated for hours in Luke 14:26-33. I knew there was something very special for me in those verses. The desire of my heart was to be a disciple of Jesus. It was during this intense meditation that Jesus crooked his finger at me and said, "Follow me!" I instantly obeyed!

What a thrill it was when God was putting Frances and me together for a ministry he planned for us, when he said to Frances, "1969 was Jeanne's (Charles' deceased wife), 1970 is yours. Start it off right the first minute at the Party for the Lord." God had spoken with voiceless knowledge into her mind exactly when we were to be married.

Why had God been so present that she could hear his voiceless words? Because in total dependence on him she cried out with all her heart for his answer as to when to get married. She did this only because she wanted to obey God.

Then, as only God can do, that same night, 1200 miles away, that same God spoke into my mind in reply to a yearning only to obey his every wish. He said to me, "You and Frances are to be married at the New Year's Eve Party for the Lord at midnight, to start the fabulous 1970 year."

I didn't question God.

I didn't even consider whether or not I had heard God speak. I knew, without a doubt, that God told me what he wanted me to do, and I obeyed God!

There is always a reward when we obey God. We married in obedience to him, without ever having dated each other! God's reward for obedience has been a marriage completely made in heaven!

Only a few months before that, God had instructed me to cut down my accounting practice time to fifty per cent. As soon as the time was right, I told my

partners exactly what God had said. There was no
question in my mind about doing it, even though he
had given me no reason, or indication of what he
wanted me to do with the time. There was no hint or
purpose of any kind.

I didn't argue.

I didn't question his purpose.

I just knew he said to do it, and so I did.

I obeyed God.

God's reward? He gave Frances to me and a ministry
with her that took up almost exactly half of our time
for the first two years.

In February, 1973, God spoke again. He told both of
us that I was to cut down my accounting pracitce time
to one-fourth. Without questioning why or how we
could financially afford it, we told my partners what
God had said and immediately made arrangements to
reduce my time in the firm.

We only wanted to do what God said, so we
instantly obeyed.

The reward? God enlarged our ministry, added a new
healing dimension and put us on television after giving
us the time to do it!

In September, 1975, we were walking through the
Chicago O'Hare airport, holding hands, but not talking
to each other. Suddenly God spoke. I turned to Frances
and said, "God just told me to retire from my accounting practice!" Frances turned and said, "That's what he
just said to me!"

Neither of us doubted that God had spoken, so we
knew we had to obey. We made retirement
arrangements as soon as we returned to Houston and I
was fully retired by the end of September.

The reward? God again enlarged our ministry and today there would be absolutely no time to do any accounting work of any kind, because we are completely submerged in the will and work of God!

We marvel at the hundreds of times God spoke to his people in the Old and New Testaments. He gave us his Holy Spirit so he could speak to us from within by this very portion of God himself living within us. What an awesome thing it is to know that God can constantly speak to us — if we want to listen.

People often get so involved in just living that they don't take time to sit down and listen for that still small voice of God. It's in the quiet moments that he gives his greatest directives for our lives — if we will be still and know that he is God! (See Psalm 46:10).

It was through total and complete commitment of our lives that we learned to recognize the voiceless voice of God. It is when we obey without questioning why? how? where? when? or how much? that we can hear God speak to us.

What, then, is obedience?

Obedience is a privilege given by God.

Obedience is a command by God.

Obedience is trusting God.

Obedience is showing our love to God.

Obedience is honoring God.

Obedience is pleasing God.

Obedience is not a trial.

Obedience is not hard.

Obedience is not a punishment.

Obedience is not a burden.

What is our part in obedience? DO IT!

What is God's part? He has already done his part by writing his promises for us in his holy word.

How do we find out what to obey? By reading the word of God.

Obedience isn't sacrificing anything. It's just falling in line with God's wishes and flowing in the stream of his power and love!

OBEDIENCE LEADS TO THIS WAY UP!
DO IT!

WHAT, ME HEAL THE SICK?

(by Charles)

Who heals the sick?
  Does God?
    Does Jesus?
      Does the Holy Spirit?
      Do people?
Let's find out together!

Years ago, Frances discovered she was blind in her left eye as a result of an automobile accident. Cataracts had formed over the lens of her eye and cut off her vision.

How did she get healed?

Sight was restored in one eye by removing the lens surgically and providing a man-made lens, resulting in 20-15 vision. When another cataract formed, God divinely removed the cataract from her right eye, giving her natural 20-20 vision.

Four years later, after she had written *Hot Line to Heaven.* the exciting story of how God had restored the vision in her right eye while she was under a dryer in a beauty parlor, another cataract formed on the divinely-healed eye.

Many questions came to our mind!

Why would God heal the eye, only to let the problem reappear 4 years later?

We didn't know the answer.

We didn't know how to stand on the word of God and keep the healing!

She was prayed for by several Christians with tremendous healing ministries, but the cataract remained. We prayed to the best of our ability, but nothing happened!

After a year of prayer, an ophthalmologist recommended she have the second lens removed for what he called "happier vision." We finally consented, and she now has 20-10 vision in that eye, which is termed "miracle" vision!

A few years later an unusual problem occurred in her right eye. After we prayed, we went to an eye specialist to find out what had happened. They discovered a horseshoe-shaped tear in the eye. The doctor did not even want her to come home, and insisted she go to the hospital immediately; the tear was critical. She could permanently lose her sight at any time. We prayed, but chose to come home and have her anointed and prayed for by the elders of our church.

The tear remained critical, so she had a "cryo" or "gluing down" done on both eyes. Her recovery was miraculous! In less than three weeks she was back on the read again. She has perfect vision in that eye, although it is still without a normal lens.

Frances believes that God will, during a miracle service, give her back her human lens. She has great faith for this creative miracle and is often shocked to find that it has not happened when the power of God is being displayed mightily when hundreds with blindness, deafness, and all kinds of other diseases and afflictions are healed. We lay the same hands on her eyes that the healing power goes through to bring sight to others. We praise God often and thank Jesus often for her sight, and for the replacement of the lens she expects to receive as a gift from the Almighty God through Jesus, the Great Physician.

We are constantly meditating in the word of God to find those hidden secrets which are in plain view when the Spirit reveals simple ways to accomplish the work of Jesus.

Frances had an enlarged heart with a hole in it, and dangerously high blood pressure just a few years ago. She was having great difficulty with her blood pressure and with violent headaches resulting from it. We applied every method of prayer and every way we had learned through which God heals the sick, but nothing happened! The condition grew worse and attacks came more frequently. Then, during one of the times when she was suffering intensely from headaches, with a blood pressure of 225/140 after two-and-one-half hours of blood pressure medication,

GOD SPOKE!

I sprang to my feet, stood over Frances and took authority and dominion over her heart.

I began speaking to the heart, commanding it to be healed, to reduce to normal size.

I commanded the blood pressure to drop to normal.

For twelve minutes I spoke with authority and belief *without a doubt* BECAUSE I KNEW I HAD HEARD

GOD TELL ME TO TAKE AUTHORITY OVER THE HEART!

The heart was healed!

The doctor found it to be normal size, with no evidence of a hole. Her blood pressure has been normal ever since! The doctor said she has the heart of a sixteen-year-old girl. Glory to God!

What was the difference between the eyes and the heart?

Was it a lack of faith on my part, or Frances'?

Was it a lack of understanding of the word of God?

Does God have different plans or reasons for doing the healings differently?

I want to quote a paragraph from my book, *Follow Me,* in which I share the details of Frances' heart healing. This one paragraph is still the desire of our hearts.

> I intend to search for, live for, experiment to attain a greater measure of the phenomenal power I believe God wants us to use for his glory. I intend to test him, try him and let him prove his promise that he will open the windows of heaven even more in communicating his desires to us!

We believe God wants to heal everyone. We believe he wants everyone to live in perfect health when they serve him. We haven't found all the ways to heal the sick and afflicted, but we are learning more all the time. As we learn new ways, we test them, try them and God proves them by bringing forth more and more mighty miracles with his healing power! Jesus healed the sick by using many different methods.

We want to share a few of the ways to heal the sick, and a few principles we have learned. We believe this will help to open your mind and faith to discover by revelation of the Holy Spirit the different ways Jesus healed.

When we went to the ophthalmologist, he was very excited about a new piece of equipment just installed in his office. It was a laser beam. He explained that when an eye has a tiny hole in the retina, a delicate process is necessary to close the hole. "But," he said enthusiastically, "with this laser beam, we can aim the beam at the hole and push a button and 'zap,' the hole is closed!" He was excited, but what God showed me was even more exciting to me!

It was not the ophthalmologist who closed the hole in the eye to bring healing.

It was the laser beam of light that seared the hole shut. (If my description is not technically correct, the principle I learned is!)

It was a force, an energy, a power, a laser beam that did the actual healing.

BUT THE OPHTHALMOLOGIST WAS STILL THE DOCTOR WHO APPLIED THE ENERGY WHICH ACCOMPLISHED THE HEALING!

When the woman with an issue of blood touched the hem of Jesus' garment and was healed, Jesus said he felt healing *virtue,* or power, go from his body. (See Mark 5:30.)

Jesus is the Great Physician.

He applied the healing power, just as the ophthalmologist did. But according to Jesus, HE did not provide the healing virtue, or power, or energy which healed.

What was the source of this power which did the miracle which no physician had been able to accomplish?

Is that power available for us to use at will?

Is it available for us to use upon special occasions?

Is it available only to specially chosen ones with the gifts of healing?

Can anyone have this power? Can it be used anytime we want?

If it is a power which can be harnessed, to apply as a doctor would apply medication or surgery, then can it be used to accomplish divine health and to heal all people everywhere?

Let's look at the perfect, infallible, everlasting word of God for the discovery of the source of this power.

Jesus had just healed a man with a deformed hand. His enemies were accusing him of being possessed by Satan, king of demons, and were saying that was why demons obeyed him. Jesus replied that if Satan was fighting against himself, how could he accomplish anything? Then Jesus said Satan must be bound before his demons are cast out. Jesus further said they were saying he did his miracles by Satan's power, instead of acknowledging it was by the Holy Spirit's power. (See Mark 3:22-30).

BY WHAT POWER?

Jesus said he did the miracle by the HOLY SPIRIT'S power.

That is a fact. That is an unchangeable fact. That is truth, because Jesus is truth and the word of God is truth!

> *Therefore tell the descendants of Israel*
> *that I (God) will use MY MIGHTY*

POWER AND PERFORM GREAT MIRACLES to deliver them from slavery, and make them free (Ex. 6:6).

Whose power?

God's power!

For what?

To perform great miracles!

If you refuse, the POWER OF GOD will send a deadly plague to destroy your cattle, horses, donkeys, camels, flocks, and herds (Ex. 9:2,3).

WHOSE POWER? THE POWER OF GOD!

The HOLY SPIRIT shall come upon you, and the POWER OF GOD shall overshadow you (Luke 1:35).

I baptize only with water; but some- one is coming soon who has far higher authority than mine; in fact, I am not even worthy of being his slave. He will baptize you with fire — with the HOLY SPIRIT (Luke 3:16).

"John baptized you with water," he reminded them, "but you shall be bap- tized with the HOLY SPIRIT in just a few days" (Acts 1:5).

But when the HOLY SPIRIT has come upon you, you will receive POWER to testify about me with great effect . . . (Acts 1:8).

. . . . and the HOLY SPIRIT in the form of a dove settled upon him (Jesus) . . . (Luke 3:22).

Then Jesus, full of the HOLY SPIRIT . . . (Luke 4:1).

Then Jesus returned to Galilee, full of the Holy Spirit's POWER (Luke 4:14).

Everyone was trying to touch him, for when they did HEALING POWER went out from him and they were cured (Luke 6:19).

Jesus had just cast out a demon: *Awe gripped the people as they saw this display of the POWER OF GOD (Luke 9:43).*

This miracle at Cana in Galilee was Jesus' first public demonstration of his HEAVEN-SENT POWER. And his disciples believed that he really was the Messiah (John 2:11).

Jesus' disciples saw him do many other miracles besides the ones told about in this book, but these are recorded so that you will believe that he is the Messiah, the Son of God, and that believing in him you will have life (John 20:30,31).

The words I say are not my own but are from my Father who lives in me. And HE DOES HIS WORK THROUGH ME (John 14:10).

O men of Israel, listen! God publicly endorsed Jesus of Nazareth by DOING TREMENDOUS MIRACLES THROUGH HIM, as you well know (Acts 2:22).

I have won them by my message and by the good way I have lived before them, and by the MIRACLES DONE

THROUGH ME as signs from God —
ALL BY THE HOLY SPIRIT'S POWER
(Rom. 15:19).

It is clear, then, from the scriptures given, that

. . . all miracles come from God;

. . . God's Holy Spirit is the power;

. . . God is the source of this power;

. . . God releases his healing power through people, first in the New Testament through Jesus, then the disciples, and makes that same healing power available to all of us who believe.

Frances and I prayed for the sick for several years, but only occasionally one would be healed. We couldn't understand why. Then came the baptism with the Holy Spirit. We received power, just like the disciples did when they received the baptism with the Holy Spirit on the Day of Pentecost, and people started getting healed in our meetings! It was not until we received the baptism with the Holy Spirit and spoke in tongues that power to heal came into us. And, just as it did through Jesus (Luke 6:19 above), healing power went out from us and people were healed. God's Holy Spirit Power to heal comes out of a person baptized with the Holy Spirit, and God heals through people. (See the last three scriptures quoted above.)

For a few months the healings came as we laid hands on people and prayed for them. Then one day God taught us something new that greatly increased the number who got healed. As soon as we prayed for a man who could hardly walk or stand, we said, "Pick up your cane and walk."

He took one slow, hesitating step, and didn't fall over!

Then he took another,

. . . and another. In moments he was walking all over the high school stage where we were praying!

We discovered if someone did something to find out if they were healed, they often were! But if they didn't test their body to see if they were healed, often there were no results. Then we discovered that Jesus and the disciples did this many times.

Stretch forth your hand! (Matthew 12:13).

Pick up your bed and walk! (Mark 2:11).

Go wash the clay off your eyes! (John 9:6,7).

Faith doesn't accomplish very much without action!

Then suddenly in February, 1973, God healed about fifty people of all kinds of diseases and afflictions in one service! Simultaneously, people started falling under the power of God as we touched them. What was different than before?

We have since learned that the virtue, or healing power which came out of Jesus, comes out of our hands stronger than it does any other part of our bodies. Many times we can actually feel it surge into another individual. When they feel the power, they realize something supernatural is happening to them. Many times that "something supernatural" becomes a faith contact, and healing takes place.

That power is in us because we are filled with the Holy Spirit!

The Bible says we received power when we accepted the baptism with the Holy Spirit!

We believe it!

The Bible says that signs and wonders will follow!

We believe it!

We notice the flow of energy or power coming out of us most plainly when we lay hands on people and they fall under the power or are touched by the slaying power of the Holy Spirit! Some people call it being "slain in the Spirit!" It is totally supernatural. We have nothing to do with it except the Holy Spirit in us flows out through our hands and sometimes through all of our body.

We have seen as many as eight hundred people fall at one time, as the wind of the Holy Spirit swept through an auditorium like a rushing mighty wind. We have raised our hands and have seen several hundred fall backwards at one time. We have even heard the sound of the Spirit, moving with great power when hundreds have fallen backwards to the floor, slain by the mighty power of God's Holy Spirit.

The simplest way we can describe this power is to say it moves like a wind or energy out through our hands and goes into the people we touch. Thousands have been healed this way! Praise Jesus!

Are we any different from anyone else?

No. We are just like millions of twentieth century believers who have received the baptism with the Holy Spirit and speak in tongues. Any one of them, *if they believe,* can experience the same thing! Hallelujah!

Jesus put it so simply. He was talking only to believers as he gave his final Great Commission in Mark 16:15-20. After telling them to go into all the world and preach the Good News to everyone, everywhere, he gave five commands:

1. And those who believe shall use my authority to cast out demons. . .

2. . . . and they shall speak new languages.

*3. They will be able even to handle
snakes with safety,
4. and if they drink anything poisonous,
it won't hurt them. . .
5. . . . and they will be able to place
their hands on the sick and heal them.*

Let's look back at this series of commands, thinking about them in relation to healing.

Demons are cast out by the authority of Jesus. We are to cast them out; that's our part. Jesus did it while he was on earth, but he told us to do it after he went back to heaven.

Jesus commanded us to speak in new languages. That was what Frances and I did in 1972 when we received the baptism with the Holy Spirit and the healing power came into us.

We believe God would protect us if we were accidentally bitten by a snake or drank something poisonous. Because of the constant references throughout the Bible about the devil being a snake, and the poisonous creatures being evil, we believe this refers to the power of the Holy Spirit to handle Satan and his demon powers. Jesus simply says if we want to rob Satan's kingdom (his demon powers) we must first bind Satan with the power of the Holy Spirit and by the authority of Jesus.

The most simple part of the Great Commission was when Jesus said of those who believe, ". . . and they will be able to place their hands on the sick and heal them." The King James Version says, "they shall lay hands on the sick, and they shall recover."

That is super simple. There are no excess words by Jesus. There are no gimmicks or tricks. There was no instruction to pray, or to say anything. He simply said we could lay hands on the sick and they would recover! How can this be? Be sure to meet all the conditions first and then it will work for those who do.

A minister friend asked me if it was a special faith that caused almost all people to fall under the power when we lay hands on them; do we just expect them to be touched; or what causes the large percentage to fall.

Think about what the cause is this way: An electric light switch, when turned to the "off" position, breaks the circuit, or stops the flow of electrical energy between the power plant and the light bulb. When the switch is turned "on", the energy flows unhindered.

The "power," or "energy" of the Holy Spirit is in us, and when our hands touch a person's head or other part of their body, we know that the energy of God flows into the receptive person, causing them to fall backwards. When we turn "on" the switch by touching a person, we expect the power to be effective to minister to the needs of the person touched.

In the same simple way, we expect them to be healed because that same power is the healing power, energy, or virtue which goes into them. We don't understand why all are not healed, but we continue to expect them to be.

Do you have faith enough to put your hand on somebody's head or other part of their body? That's what we do. If you are endued with that same Holy Spirit power by receiving the baptism with the Holy Spirit, you can get people healed by turning the virtue "on" through you!

TRY IT!

Jesus said "those who believe." Believe what? First of all, believe in Jesus as their Savior and Lord. Believe in him for who he is — the Son of God who died to redeem us from our sins, and was resurrected by the power of the Holy Spirit!

Believe in the Holy Spirit and in receiving this enduement of power the same way God prescribed it in the New Testament. Those believers — the 120, including the disciples, Jesus' mother and others — all began doing one thing.

> *And everyone present was filled with the*
> *Holy Spirit and began speaking in lan-*
> *guages they didn't know, for the Holy*
> *Spirit gave them this ability (Acts 2:4).*

They ALL began to speak in languages they didn't know! Some people attempt to get this healing power in other ways. They don't believe in speaking in tongues. That makes them disbelievers, not one of *"those who believe,"* so therefore they do not meet the scriptural conditions Jesus required for them to be able to lay hands on the sick to heal them.

Jesus then said in the Great Commission that those who believe would speak new languages. Again, if a person doesn't believe in speaking new languages, he disqualifies himself as a believer to this extent.

A few were healed before we received the baptism because we prayed, but it didn't happen very much, and it wasn't because we laid hands on them with power. There was no power which could come out of us to heal them.

Once the power resided in us after receiving the baptism with the Holy Spirit, and we laid hands on the sick, we saw signs and wonders follow our ministry wherever we went. We even had healings in airport

restrooms, in offices, on the streets, in cafeterias, in
parking lots, and in many places. We didn't have to
wait for an anointing to come on us because we
believed the Holy Spirit was in us and that we had
power! The Bible didn't put conditions on where or
when. It just said to lay hands on the sick and heal
them. We have even had scores of people healed while
we were sick, because Jesus didn't say to heal them
while we felt like it.

We began to discover other ways to apply this healing
power. We noticed that people would be healed if we
did certain things. For example, the deaf were not
getting healed for awhile after God opened the healing
ministry to us. We couldn't figure out why, so we asked
God about it. It wasn't long before he revealed to us
that deafness was often caused by evil spirits attaching
themselves to the ear mechanism and thereby pre-
venting the person from hearing. We noticed then that
the Bible said Jesus commanded the deaf spirit to come
out, and the man could hear.

How about that!

That sounded simple, and Jesus said we should use
his authority and cast out demons. God allowed a
young woman to come to our home who was deaf in
one ear. We tried this new formula, and it worked! Out
came the deaf demon, and the lady could hear.

We also learned that one time Jesus put his fingers in
a person's ears and said, "Open." That person was
healed. We try to ask people what caused their deafness
before we pray. Then we either cast a demon out or
use the authority of Jesus to heal the ear, depending on
what the cause was.

One time we just held our hands on a man's ears
who had no eardrums, let the power of God go through

our fingers into the ears, and asked God to create new eardrums. Guess what! He did!! God put new eardrums in both ears, and the man heard normally. We didn't have to work at all to get that fantastic creative miracle done! It was simply done by the power of God's Holy Spirit.

We have discovered that as a general rule, diseases described by physicians as incurable are caused by demons. First, we noticed Jesus cast out demons when a person was deaf, dumb, blind, insane, or had other incurable diseases or afflictions. We found the scripture that said,

> *Last of all I want to remind you that your strength must come from the LORD'S MIGHTY POWER WITHIN YOU. Put on all of God's armor so that you will be able to stand safe against all strategies and tricks of Satan. For we are not fighting against people made of flesh and blood, but against persons without bodies — the evil rulers of the unseen world, those mighty satanic beings and great evil princes of darkness who rule this world; and against huge numbers of wicked spirits in the spirit world (Eph. 6:10-12).*

You see, doctors who are not baptized with the Holy Spirit cannot see nor understand these unseen spirits, and so they have no way to fight them. We believe in doctors, and praise God for their calling. But, if they don't meet the conditions of a believer, they do not have the power nor understand how to deal with these "persons without bodies."

A person who believes and meets the conditions of receiving the power and gifts of the Holy Spirit can discern these evil creatures and cast them out with Jesus' authority, so people with incurable diseases can be healed! People can be set free from the bondages evil spirits bring through sickness and attachment to people's minds.

Some of the diseases we run into that are mostly caused by spirits are cancer, diabetes, arthritis, multiple sclerosis, deafness, dumbness, and blindness. Just as Jesus healed two kinds of deafness, there are conditions not caused by spirits which apparently result in forms of these diseases.

A lady in Colorado came for healing one day. She had a pain in her side which had existed for about three years. She had been to all kinds of doctors, psychologists, preachers, and had been prayed for, but the pain persisted. With all those facts, I reasoned that it must be a spirit, so I simply said, "Satan I bind you. You spirit of pain, come out." It did. The pain left instantly. When I asked her what happened, she said it was like a leech with little legs dug into her that suddenly turned loose, turned away from her and left through the air! I didn't see it, but the results were evident that the spirit left her.

Jesus simply told fever to leave Peter's mother-in-law. It left and she was healed. (See Luke 4:38.) We have done the same thing, because Jesus said we could, and he gave us the same power he received. We often command pain or fever to leave a body and it leaves. It's exciting to see the awesome power of God at work!

Jesus spoke as a man with authority. He told the storm to stop. It did! The waves calmed at once!

One day a woman about sixty years old came up to the book table where we were autographing books after a miracle service. She had an eight-pound tumor which made her look nine months pregnant. I simply commanded the tumor to leave. She fell under the power of God, then got up dancing and shouting! It was like she had delivered an eight-pound baby, because you couldn't find the tumor! It was there and instantly it wasn't there! It vanished, disappearing because of the power of God.

I don't understand it. Nor do I understand how God spoke the universe into existance! It is by the same power of his Holy Spirit that all things are done. He even makes things out of what doesn't exist! He is an exciting God to serve, and I love to be where the action is! That's where Peter and James and John were. God let me know that we are no different now than they were then, and that he isn't any different either!

He gets rid of sin in our lives in the same way he got rid of that eight-pound tumor. When we really want to serve him, and honestly and sincerely ask him to forgive us of all our sins, he does. The sin is there and immediately it's not there. He removes it by the power of the Holy Spirit and by the provision Jesus made when he shed his blood to wash away our sins.

There are other ways in the Bible to heal the sick. If we apply those scriptures and believe, they will work too.

You can pray for yourself and get healed according to James 5:13. You can get the elders of your church to anoint you with oil, and the prayer of faith will heal you. That's found in James 5:14,15. You can anoint a cloth, have it laid on someone miles away and they will get healed if you believe without a doubt. That is told in Acts 19:11,12.

When we are worshipping God in a service and get sick people to begin praising God instead of thinking about themselves, the power of God falls and people get healed all over an audience! Recently the power was so strong that a baby in the nursery was healed of an umbilical hernia that protruded one and one-half inches. Instantly it went in.

Sometimes thirty, forty or fifty at a time will get healed of one disease or affliction. We have seen as many as two hundred arthritis victims healed at one time when the power of God fell and God informed us with a word of knowledge that he was healing arthritis in mass!

We stand in awe as we minister to audiences of all sizes when God begins to give us word of knowledge for various diseases or afflictions and begins to heal people all over the audience. It never ceases to amaze us the way he does these miracles!

His purpose in doing all these mighty miracles, healings and signs and wonders is so that people will believe! He often causes atheists to believe in Jesus and accept him as their Savior. Sometimes the hardest ones for God to get to believe are the Christians who do not believe in the supernatural. But he is causing millions in these last days before the return of Jesus to believe in the unlimited power he is displaying today.

DO YOU BELIEVE *YOU* CAN HEAL THE SICK?

LAY HANDS ON THEM — THAT'S YOUR PART.

GOD WILL DO MIGHTY MIRACLES AND WILL ALWAYS DO HIS PART, IF YOU DO YOUR PART!

And being fully persuaded that, what he had promised, he was able also to perform (Romans 4:21 KJV).

THIS WAY UP!

DO YOU NEED HEALING?

Take these promises of God like medicine, and continue taking large doses until healed. Follow the same prescription to maintain a healing!

PRESCRIPTION FOR HEALING

Bless the Lord, O my soul, and forget not all his benefits: Who forgiveth all thine iniquities; who healeth ALL thy diseases (Psalm 103:2,3).

NOT SOME, BUT ALL OF MY DISEASES ARE HEALED!

My son, attend to my words; incline thine ear unto my sayings.

Let them not depart from thine eyes; keep them in the midst of thine heart.

For they are LIFE unto those that find them, and HEALTH to all their flesh (Proverbs 4:20-22).

LIFE AND HEALTH ARE MINE, HALLELUJAH!

Let thine heart retain my words: keep my commandments, and live (Proverbs 4:4).

THANK YOU, FATHER. I'M GOING TO LIVE BECAUSE I'M RETAINING YOUR WORDS!

The curse of the Lord is in the house of the wicked: but he blesseth the habitation of the just (Proverbs 3:33).

IF I AM BLESSED, I AM NO LONGER SICK! GLORY!!

Now therefore hearken unto me, O ye children: for blessed (and healthy) *are they that keep my ways (Proverbs 8:32).*

I'M BLESSED AND HEALTHY! PRAISE GOD!

For whoso findeth me findeth life, and shall obtain the favour of the Lord (Proverbs 8:35).

PRAISE THE LORD, NOT ONLY DO I HAVE HEALTH; I ALSO HAVE FAVOUR WITH GOD!

The labour of the righteous tendeth to LIFE: the fruit of the wicked to sin (Proverbs 10:16).

PRAISE THE LORD, MY WORK SHALL BRING ME LIFE!

The fear of the Lord prolongeth days: but the years of the wicked shall be shortened (Proverbs 10:27).

HALLELUJAH, I'M GOING TO LIVE A LONG LIFE!

The way of the Lord is strength to the upright: but destruction shall be to the workers of iniquity (Proverbs 10:29).

PRAISE GOD BECAUSE I AM WALKING WITH THE LORD, I HAVE STRENGTH!

There is that speaketh like the piercings of a sword: but the tongue of the wise is HEALTH! (Proverbs 12:18).

MY TONGUE SPEAKS HEALTH!

A wholesome tongue is a tree of life: but perverseness therein is a breach in the spirit (Proverbs 15:4).

MY TONGUE SPEAKS THE WORD OF GOD! HALLELUJAH!

The light of the eyes rejoiceth the heart: and a good report maketh the bones fat (Proverbs 15:30).

I'M GOING TO KEEP MAKING GOOD REPORTS!

Pleasant words are as an honeycomb, sweet to the soul, and health to the bones (Proverbs 16:24).

LORD, I'M WATCHING MY WORDS SO MY BONES WILL BE HEALTHY.

A merry heart doeth good like a medicine: but a broken spirit drieth the bones (Proverbs 17:22).

THANK YOU, LORD, FOR MY MERRY HEART!

Death and life are in the power of the tongue: and they that love it shall eat the fruit thereof (Proverbs 18:21).

LORD, I'M WATCHING MY WORDS CAREFULLY!

The fear of the Lord tendeth to life: and he that hath it shall abide satisfied; he shall not be visited with evil (Proverbs 19:23).

PRAISE GOD, REVERENCE OF THE LORD BRINGS HEALTH!

By humility and the fear of the Lord are riches, and honour, and life (Proverbs 22:4).

HALLELUJAH, ALL THESE ARE MINE!

Blessed is the man that walketh not in the counsel of the ungodly, nor standeth in the way of sinners, nor sitteth in the seat of the scornful. But his delight is in the law of the Lord; and in his law doth he meditate day and night. And he shall be like a tree planted by the rivers of water, that bringeth forth his fruit in his season; HIS LEAF ALSO SHALL NOT WITHER; and whatsoever he doeth shall prosper (Psalm 1:1-3).

ONLY A SICK LEAF WITHERS, THEREFORE BE-CAUSE I WALK NOT IN THE COUNSEL OF THE UNGODLY, I SHALL NOT BE SICK! AND I'M GOING TO PROSPER BESIDES! HALLELUJAH!

The Lord will give strength unto his people; the Lord will bless his people with peace (Psalm 29:11).

GLORY TO GOD FOR HIS STRENGTH!

O Lord my God, I cried unto thee, and thou hast healed me (Psalm 30:2).

THANK YOU, LORD, FOR HEARING MY PRAYER.

For the Lord God is a sun and shield: the Lord will give grace and glory: no good thing will be withhold from them that walk uprightly (Psalm 84:11).

NOTHING WILL BE WITHHELD FROM ME, INCLUDING MY HEALING!

He sent his word, and healed them (Psalm 107:20).

PRAISE GOD FOR HIS WORD!

He healeth the broken in heart, and bindeth up their wounds (Psalm 147:3).

PRAISE GOD I'M HEALED!

And the prayer of faith shall save the sick, and the Lord shall raise him up (James 5:15).

LORD, I PRAY THE PRAYER OF FAITH!

Who his own self bare our sins in his own body on the tree, that we, being dead to sins, should live unto righteousness: by whose stripes ye were healed (I Peter 2:24).

I WAS HEALED!

And Jesus went about all Galilee, teaching in their synagogues, and preaching the gospel of the kingdom, and healing all manner of sickness and all manner of disease among the people (Matthew 4:23).

HE HEALED ALL MANNER OF SICKNESS, AND HE IS STILL HEALING!

I will take sickness away from the midst of thee (Exodus 23:25).

THANK YOU FOR THIS PROMISE!

But he was wounded for our transgressions, he was bruised for our iniquities: the chastisement of our peace was upon him; and with his stripes we are healed (Isaiah 53:5).

I AM HEALED!

But unto you that fear my name shall the Sun of righteousness arise with healing in his wings (Malachi 4:2).

THANK YOU, LORD, FOR THE HEALING IN HIS WINGS!

Then he called his twelve disciples together, and gave them power and authority over all devils, and to cure diseases. And he sent them to preach the kingdom of God, and to heal the sick (Luke 9:1,2).

THANK YOU FOR THAT POWER!

I shall not die, but live, and declare the works of the Lord (Psalm 118:17).

AND I'LL KEEP ON DECLARING HIS WORKS!

Behold, I am the Lord, the God of all flesh: is there any thing too hard for me? (Jeremiah 32:27).

PRAISE GOD, NOTHING IS TOO HARD FOR HIM.

Think of it! The Lord healed me! (Isaiah 38:20 TLB).

HALLELUJAH!

If thou wilt diligently hearken to the voice of the Lord thy God, and wilt do that which is right in his sight, and wilt give ear to his commandments, and keep all his statutes, I will put none of these diseases upon thee, which I have brought upon the Egyptians; for I am the Lord that healeth thee (Exodus 15:26).

THANK YOU THAT WE HAVE BEEN REDEEMED FROM THE CURSE!

PRAISE GOD WE HAVE HIS WORD
FOR HEALTH AND HEALING!
SAY IT!!!

I NEARLY MISSED HEAVEN!

(by Frances)

Do you think God has a sense of humor? I feel he must have, because he made me! Many of the things that have happened in our ministry have a humorous beginning, and our teaching on forgiveness started in a most unusual way!

Charles and I had been extremely busy just before Thanksgiving and had an extra hard schedule. We had flown to St. Louis, Missouri, then to Minnesota, then to Eugene, Oregon, and then back to Houston in time to make another flying trip to western Texas, then to Los Angeles and return.

We were exhausted! Instead of staying overnight in Los Angeles and coming home the next day, we took a night flight and arrived home about three o'clock in the morning. We were completely worn out because the schedule had been so grueling. We had prayed for a tremendous amount of flu and virus infections and had really been exposed to an unusual amount of communicable diseases. God has always protected us. But there are certain natural laws of God which must be obeyed, and when we over-extend our bodies, there is a price to be paid.

We live in divine health about ninety-eight per cent of the time. But every once in a while the devil takes a real good swing at us — and connects — when we're exhausted!

Who would ever believe that someone in the miracle ministry occasionally gets sick? Well, we do!

After arriving home at three o'clock in the morning, we would have had no problems, but . . .

WE HAD TO GET UP EARLY THE NEXT MORNING because we were scheduled to make a series of TV programs. We had to get the formats typed so we dragged ourselves out of bed and went to the TV studio. Making TV programs under the extremely hot lights is not the easiest thing in the world, especially when you make six or seven in one day. Usually when Charles and I finish a taping session, we are so exhausted, we literally crawl to the local cafeteria to eat our dinner and get home and in bed as fast as we can. Usually on TV day, this is by six or seven o'clock in the evening.

This day was different, however, because Graham and Treena Kerr were to be our special guests on TV, so we made two extra programs. To further complicate matters, we were having a banquet at our church that same night where Graham was going to speak on *How to Cook with New Wine*. Members of our staff and friends prepared the meal. Because they weren't accustomed to serving between seven and eight hundred people, it took longer than anticipated. We all didn't get fed until around nine o'clock, so the program began to run behind schedule.

The meeting was beautiful! Around eleven-thirty at night, it was drawing to a close when someone came to us and asked, "Did you make arrangements for the kitchen crew to come in and clean up the hall and the kitchen?"

Someone had forgotten to notify them, so we had to clean the kitchen! The next day was Thanksgiving, when he hold our biggest meeting of the year. People from all over the world come to worship the Lord with us, so all the staff and members of the board of directors had to pitch in to get the kitchen cleaned up!

Did you ever try to clean up a kitchen where pots and pans are big enough to cook food for almost a thousand people? We all started, but Charles insisted I go home and take Graham and Treena, so we wouldn't be exhausted! This I did, but Charles stayed until the last dish was washed and put away. He didn't get home until around 3 o'clock in the morning! THIS WOULD HAVE BEEN ALL RIGHT, BUT . . .

WE HAD TO GET UP EARLY THE NEXT MORNING because it was Thanksgiving Day, and our phone rings off the wall with calls from people who are coming in from out-of-town for the service, wanting to know where their motel reservations are, and if someone is going to meet them. Our staff was calling to find out how to make the minimum number of trips to the airport. There are always many questions to answer concerning the sound system and all the many little details on the day of a meeting.

THAT WOULD HAVE BEEN ALL RIGHT, if we could have taken a nap in the afternoon, but on Thanksgiving Day we meet at one of the local restaurants from two until four o'clock and fellowship with our out-of-town guests. We had a beautiful time with Graham and Treena and the other guests, and THAT WOULD HAVE BEEN ALL RIGHT, too, except we didn't have time for a nap before church time, because we start the service as soon as the sanctuary is packed. This often happens an hour before actual starting time.

Graham and Treena shared their testimony of how God had reached down and touched their lives. Many people wanted to be ministered to at the end of the service, and we didn't leave until after midnight. THAT WOULD HAVE BEEN ALL RIGHT, BUT . . .

WE HAD TO GET UP EARLY THE NEXT MORNING because Graham and Treena had to catch a seven o'clock plane for a meeting, so we had to get out of bed at five!

THAT WOULD HAVE BEEN ALL RIGHT if we would have come back home and gone to bed. But after we've been out of town, our stack of mail is mountainous, so we plowed right in and before we knew it, it was one o'clock the next morning! THAT WOULD HAVE BEEN ALL RIGHT, BUT . . .

WE HAD TO GET UP EARLY THE NEXT MORNING because we had a speaking date in Denver at two in the afternoon.

In our house, Charles is high octane at five o'clock in the morning. He gets out of bed, loves Jesus, and dances before the Lord all the way to the bathroom to shave, sings in the shower, and generally has a wonderful time with Jesus before he comes back out to wake me up. I'm high octane at midnight or later, but I'm not so hot at five in the morning! I usually pull the cover over my head and hope Charles doesn't remember I'm under the pile! (It hasn't worked yet, but I'm still trying!)

This morning was different, however!

When the alarm went off, Charles shut it off, rolled over and touched me, and said, "Honey, I feel sick!" If you want to see someone suddenly become high octane, you should see me when Charles says something like that! I sat up in bed, laid hands on him so hard it should have shaken anything out of him, and said, "I rebuke that in the name of Jesus!"

Charles said, "I still feel sick!"

I laid hands on him again and said, "I rebuke that in the name of Jesus!"

Charles said, "I've never been so sick in my life."

I said, "Take the name of Jesus for strength to get out of bed!"

Charles said "Jesus" the weakest I ever heard anyone say it, and got out of bed. But he certainly didn't dance before the Lord on the way to shave and shower that morning.

By this time he had chills and fever, and was shaking all over the place! Even though the weather in Houston was pleasant, Denver had the lowest reading in history along with record snow!! Charles bundled up in his winter coat and fake fur hat and even though it wasn't cold in Houston, he shivered all the way to the airport.

I'm surprised he wasn't black and blue by the time we got there, because I spent the entire time laying hands on him and rebuking the devil, and speaking words of healing. The more I prayed and the more I rebuked the devil, the sicker he got!

We got on the plane and Charles fell asleep. When we arrived in Denver, he was REALLY sick! Marilyn and Wally Hickey met us at the airport and I had them pray for Charles, but he was still miserable. We went directly to the Hilton Hotel, which I thought was overheated, but Charles was still shivering.

There's two tremendous advantages to ministering together. The Bible says that one can put a thousand to flight, and two can put ten thousand to flight. We'd rather put ten thousand to flight any day! Another advantage is that if one of us isn't quite up to snuff, the other one can take the entire meeting, and the one who's not up to par can sleep, and look like they're praying!

I told Charles not to worry, but to just sit at the back of the stage, and I'd take the entire service. By this time he had such chills and fever he couldn't even sit there without his coat, so an usher brought it to him. There he was all bundled up in the background as I began the service.

After some worshipping and praising the Lord, I began to speak. I hadn't talked more than three or four minutes, when the Lord spoke to me loud and clear and said, "I've got something special for Charles to do!"

I really got excited, because I knew he had healed Charles! I turned around and said, "Honey, God just told me that he has something special for you to do!"

Charles looked like I had hit him on the head with a two-by-four. HE HADN'T HEARD GOD SAY A THING! I praise the Lord for my husband, though, because one of the things we've learned is to never question what God says to the other. Charles KNEW that I had heard God, even though he hadn't heard anything. So he walked up to the pulpit, and because he didn't know what to do, he opened his Bible and began to read from the book of Romans. Part of what he read was,

> *. . . and* *CALLETH* *THOSE* *THINGS*
> *WHICH* *BE* *NOT* *AS* *THOUGH* *THEY*
> *WERE (Romans 4:17 KJV).*
>
> *And being fully persuaded that, what*
> *he had promised, he was able also to*
> *perform (Romans 4:21 KJV).*

He stopped, very carefully closed his Bible, and laid it down on the pulpit.

Charles, being a CPA, is very neat and orderly about everything. After laying his Bible down, he turned directly to me, and with his mouth in front of the microphone so everyone could hear, he made this grand announcement:

"HONEY, I'M SO SICK, I THINK I'M GOING TO VOMIT!"

Normally we speak from a very small podium or stand more often than not. But this time, God had impressed upon Marilyn and Wally Hickey to bring the huge pulpit from their church, which would have been big enough for two people to hide behind. Charles dropped down behind the pulpit!

GOD THINKS OF EVERYTHING!

On the bottom shelf of the pulpit were four glasses, three empty and one with water. Charles very carefully picked up the first glass and began to throw up! He's the only person I know of who can throw up in a glass and hit it! I'd be all over the place!

I was so mad at the devil for what he was doing, I hit Charles with all my strength and screamed, "Devil, in the name of Jesus, get your hands off my husband. He's God's property, and he doesn't belong to you!" If Charles had gone under the power, it would have been my power because I hit him so hard, and certainly not God's!

Charles kept right on vomiting!

About that time, a message in tongues came out which was one of the most powerful messages I've ever heard in my entire life.

Charles kept right on vomiting!

GUESS WHO GOT THE INTERPRETATION?

Charles did! By this time he had filled the three glasses, so he drank the glass of water, came up from behind the pulpit with such power I had to hang on to keep from falling over. He very carefully took his handkerchief, wiped his mouth and said, "Now that that's over with, I'll give you the interpretation."

If my word is true, I will perform it,
thus saith the Lord!

AND THE POWER OF GOD BROKE LOOSE!

A lady who had been sitting on one of the end seats in the front row jumped up, picked up one of the heavy chairs, lifted it over her head, and began running back and forth across the front of the auditorium!

Charles and I have only had the baptism for a few years, and we weren't used to what Pentecostals do, and couldn't imagine what was going on!

Finally, we discovered what was happening! The woman had rheumatoid arthritis, and had not even been able to lift a cup of coffee to her mouth. While Charles was throwing up, the power of God touched her, and she was instantly healed! She was so excited, the only way she could think of to tell the world was to pick up the heaviest thing she saw, which was a chair. We saw her a year later and her gnarled, twisted fingers on both hands were straight, natural and nimble, healed by the power of God.

About the time we found out what had happened to her, a woman came running down the aisle of the Hilton ballroom, tripped and fell, got up and started running again. When she got about twenty feet away from the stage, she fell backwards under the power of God! Later we found out she had been brought on a stretcher from a hospital with terminal cancer, and God healed her!

The power of God was so strong, no one could reach the stage. One time we looked over and saw three fingers hanging on to the edge of the stage, with the rest of the body draped over the stairs. The secretary of Life for Laymen was healed of osteoporosis that day, and many other remarkable healings took place.

Then the Shekinah Glory of God lifted, and the service was over! You probably think Charles was healed! HE WAS NOT! When the glory lifted, Charles was just as sick as he had ever been, so we went right back to the airport to come home. We got on the plane, Charles promptly fell asleep, and I began to read my Bible.

Normally, I ask God where to read in the Bible, or have some indication of where I should read, but this day I just opened my Bible and it "happened" to open to the sixth chapter of Matthew. My eyes caught the seventh and eighth verse, so I began to read.

> *Don't recite the same prayer over and over as the heathen do, who think prayers are answered only by repeating them again and again. Remember, your Father knows exactly what you need even before you ask him!*

I sat there and agreed with that paraphrase and thought
about the many people who say the same prayers over
and over again without realizing what they are really
saying. I began to pray for a man with whom I was
sharing one time about the virgin birth of Jesus. I said,
"The Holy Spirit enshrouded Mary and she was im-
pregnated with Jesus." He said, "Where did you get
that stupid idea?"

I knew what church he attended, so I asked him if
he had ever said the Apostles' Creed. He reminded me
that he had been in church every Sunday for twenty-
eight years and had said it every single time. I asked
him to say it for me. He started:

> "I believe in God the Father Almighty,
> Maker of heaven and earth; And in Jesus
> Christ His only Son our Lord; who was
> conceived by the Holy Ghost, born of
> the Virgin Mary . . ."

I stopped him and said, "Would you mind repeating
that last phrase again?" He looked shocked, and said,
"who was conceived by the Holy Ghost," . . . Then he
added, "I never knew that was in there!"

I reminisced about how many times I had said the
Lord's Prayer in a church service and never really
thought about a single thing I said. Have you ever done
that? I was really in agreement with what I had just
read.

I continued on,

> *Pray along these lines: "Our Father in*
> *heaven, we honor your holy name. We*
> *ask that your kingdom will come now.*

Maybe I had better stop here a moment and tell you
that I LOVE *The Living Bible!* I read all the different

translations, but for just plain enjoyment, I read *The Living Bible.* Because of its influence upon the world, I chose to put the Living New Testament and Psalms on tape. I think it's vital that you know how I feel about *The Living Bible* before I make the next comments!

I stopped reading, and said to myself, "Ken Taylor, you did such a wonderful job on the rest of *The Living Bible*, but you sure missed on the Lord's Prayer." I continued to myself, "It sounds so much more spiritual to say,

> *Our Father which art in heaven, Hallowed be thy name. Thy kingdom come. Thy will be done in earth, as it is in heaven" (KJV).*

Why do we think it sounds so much more spiritual that way? Because that's the way we learned it! I continued,

> *Give us our food again today, as usual,*

I stopped. GIVE US OUR FOOD AGAIN TODAY, AS USUAL! How unspiritual can you get? I was feeling momentary disappointment at *The Living Bible.* I thought about the way I had learned it as a child.

> *Give us this day our daily bread (KJV).*

Then I thought, doesn't the word "food" make much more sense than bread? Who wants to eat just bread every day?

I continued on,

> *and forgive us our sins,*

"That's right, Father, if there's any sin in my life that I haven't asked forgiveness for, please forgive me. I want to make sure I'm prayed up and forgiven at all times."

I continued,

> *just as we have forgiven those who have sinned against us. Don't bring us into*

*temptation, but deliver us from the Evil
One. Amen."*

I always thought the word "Amen" was the end of
something, but then I discovered that the most important part of the Lord's Prayer comes AFTER the
"Amen," because I saw something I had never seen
before that day, even though I had read it many times.

*Your heavenly Father will forgive you if
you forgive those who sin against you;
but if you refuse to forgive them, he will
not forgive you (Matthew 6:7-15).*

Those words jumped out of the page at me! IF YOU
REFUSE TO FORGIVE THEM, HE WILL NOT FOR-
GIVE YOU! Other scriptures came rushing back at me.

*Whatever you bind on earth is bound in
heaven, and whatever you free on earth
will be freed in heaven (Matthew 18:18).*

The King James says:

*Verily I say unto you, Whatsoever ye
shall bind on earth shall be bound in
heaven: and whatsoever ye shall loose on
earth shall be loosed in heaven (Matthew
18:18 KJV).*

The revelation knowledge of God came through to
reveal that we can bind individuals as well as things by
unforgiveness. I had always thought about situations
and attitudes in our lives, but had never before thought
about this scripture in relation to what we can do to
the lives of other people simply by unforgiveness!

Mark 11:23,24 is probably the best known of all the
"faith" scriptures, and I thought about the last verse.

*Listen to me! You can pray for any-
thing, and if you believe, you have it;
it's yours! (Mark 11:24).*

So many people have tried to claim that particular verse without the condition which follows it! They go together! The first one does not go into operation until you have fulfilled the last one! Look at verse 25:

> *But when you are praying, first forgive*
> *anyone you are holding a grudge against,*
> *so that your Father in heaven will for-*
> *give you for your sins too (Mark 11:25).*

Then I remembered the scripture in Luke 17:4 which tells us to forgive seventy times seven, and then start all over again.

Thoughts flashed through my mind!

How many peoples' prayers are hindered because of unforgiveness in their hearts?

How many people are not able to be healed because of an unforgiving spirit?

How many people are needlessly suffering from arthritis and similar diseases because of unforgiveness in their hearts?

How many people are going to get to the entrance of heaven and hear God say, "I can't let you in. You didn't forgive on earth, and my word says that it's impossible for me to forgive your sins because you didn't forgive your brother?"

Something had to be done to get the message out on forgiveness!

I thought of Hebrews 12:14,15.

> *Try to stay out of all quarrels and seek*
> *to live a clean and holy life, for one who*
> *is not holy will not see the Lord. Look*
> *after each other so that not one of you*
> *will fail to find God's best blessings.*

> *Watch out that no bitterness takes root among you, for as it springs up it causes deep trouble, hurting many in their spiritual lives.*

Too many people have said, "I'll forgive him, but I won't forget what he did to me," and have literally been consumed by bitterness, which can eat away at the human soul like cancer eats the body! You haven't forgiven until you have forgotten! God says in Jeremiah 31:34 *"I will forgive and forget their sins."* He also says in Isaiah 43:25 that he blots away our sins and *"will never think of them again!"* He is our example.

I thought of a story in Matthew 18:18 about the king who decided to bring his accounts up to date. One of his debtors owed him $10,000,000. That's a lot of money! When the man fell down before the king and asked forgiveness, the king forgave him his debt. God flashed into my mind the fact that this was exactly what he did the day I said, "God, forgive my sins!" Nothing could have ever repaid God for the forty-nine years of running from him that I did. Yet when I asked him to forgive me, he did! Think of this story with the king as God, and you being the debtor.

It goes on to say that a debtor of yours came and asked forgiveness of a small amount of $2,000, which is certainly small by the side of $10,000,000. You refused to forgive him. The story ends with the angry king (God) sending the man to the torture chamber until he had paid every last penny due. The story ends with a tremendous statement:

> *So shall my heavenly Father do to you if you refuse to truly forgive your brothers (Matthew 18:35).*

I believe the key word in that scripture is the word "truly." When we forgive, we need to completely forget the situation. This doesn't mean that it will never be remembered again, but it does mean that you can remember it without bitterness or a feeling of retaliation.

Then in another revelation explosion, God revealed that we could actually bind people from salvation by unforgiveness on our part, and that in forgiving we could make their salvation a reality.

> *"You stiff-necked heathen! Must you forever resist the Holy Spirit? But your fathers did, and so do you! Name one prophet your ancestors didn't persecute! They even killed the ones who predicted the coming of the Righteous One — the Messiah whom you betrayed and murdered. Yes, and you deliberately destroyed God's Laws, though you received them from the hands of angels."*
>
> *The Jewish leaders were stung to fury by Stephen's accusation, and ground their teeth in rage. But Stephen, full of the Holy Spirit, gazed steadily upward into heaven and saw the glory of God and Jesus standing at God's right hand. And he told them, "Look, I see the heavens opened and Jesus the Messiah standing beside God, at his right hand!"*

This really made them mad!

Then they mobbed him, putting their hands over their ears, and drowning out his voice with their shouts, and dragged him out of the city to stone him.

The official witnesses — the executioners — took off their coats and laid them at the feet of a young man named PAUL. (Also known as Saul.)

Saul had more authority than anyone else, because he was the most powerful man there. He could have stopped the stoning, but he chose not to lift a finger in Stephen's behalf.

And as the murderous stones came hurtling at him, Stephen prayed, "Lord Jesus, receive my spirit." And he fell to his knees, shouting, "Lord, don't charge them with this sin!" and with that, he died (Acts 7:51-60).

"Lord, I forgive them." Stephen forgave!

In forgiving, he loosed the power of salvation upon Saul, who later became the great Apostle Paul, the one who wrote the major portion of the New Testament, and the one whom many feel was the greatest apostle of all. I have often wondered if Paul would have ever been saved if Stephen had not forgiven him.

I began to think of whom I might be binding by unforgiveness on my part. Was there anyone somewhere in the past that I had never truly forgiven? I asked God to really search my heart and see if there was any kind of unforgiveness there. I wondered if there was someone whom I might be holding back from salvation because of unforgiveness on my part. I thought of unsaved friends and relatives and wondered if there was anything in my heart that might be keeping them from eternal life.

At our seminars we began sharing on forgiveness. We discovered a world of people who needed to forgive their husbands, their wives, their parents, their in-laws, their doctor, their church, their pastor, and many others. The number of salvations and deliverances that have resulted because of forgiveness have been tremendous!

Recently we received a letter which stated, "I attended your forgiveness session on Tuesday, and came forward to forgive my father and mother for rejecting me all these years. Sunday night, just five days later, they were both saved!"

> *Whatsoever ye shall bind on earth shall*
> *be bound in heaven: and whatsoever ye*
> *shall loose on earth shall be loosed in*
> *heaven (Matthew 18:18 KJV).*

Hallelujah!

Charles and I were sitting in our living room one evening and talking about the remarkable things we had seen happen through forgiveness. As always, we said, "God, if there's anyone we need to forgive, remind us." Don't ever ask God to remind you of something you don't want to be reminded of, because he'll do it.

We took a cruise one year, and as everyone knows, the sponsoring organization always gets a fee for sponsoring the tour. Ours was an extremely successful tour, and the operator owed us $12,000.00. He never gave us anything! We feel God has made us stewards of the money entrusted to us. We have a great responsibility because of this: we carefully guard all of God's funds. We were really irritated over losing the $12,000! We had a bad attitude about the entire situation, and God reminded us of it!

The minute he did, both of us instantly said, "Lord, we forgive him. We forgive him. We truly forgive him." We could hardly believe that we had bitterness in our hearts even though that sum of money is a lot to a ministry like ours.

NOW WATCH WHAT GOD DID!

> *Whatsoever ye shall loose on earth shall*
> *be loosed in heaven (KJV).*

In forgiving him, we loosed the power of God on the finances of Hunter Ministries, and exactly seven days later we received a cashier's check in the mail for $50,000.00! It was the largest donation we have ever received in the history of our ministry! Glory to God! Hallelujah!

You can loose the power of God in your life for your finances, too. Maybe someone owes you money. Forgive whoever it is! You may never get the money from them. But God is your source and will loose your finances some other way!

One of the most heartbreaking scenes of forgiveness in our meetings concerns fathers molesting their daughters. Over and over again in forgiveness services, we hear young girls, and older women say, "I forgive my father for molesting me for years!" Praise God for their forgiveness, because now they've opened the door for salvation for those men who are guilty of the world's most heinous crime. I just finished listening to a tape of a young woman who was molested by her father for eleven years. Then she spent an equal number of years literally in the pit of hell because of what this did to her mind. The thrilling part is that God healed her mind when she forgave her dad and herself!

Maybe you need to forgive

. . . a father or brother for molesting you,

. . . your husband,

. . . your wife,

. . . your mother,

. . . your father,

. . . your brothers or sisters,

. . . your boss,

. . . your pastor,

. . . your church,

. . . your doctor,

. . . someone who owes you money,

. . . the woman who stole your husband,

. . . someone who molested your child,

. . . someone who gypped you in a business deal,

. . . yourself,

. . . God.

FORGIVENESS CAN TRANSFORM YOUR LIFE.

FORGIVENESS CAN HEAL YOUR BODY.

FORGIVENESS CAN HEAL YOUR FINANCES.

FORGIVENESS CAN HEAL YOUR MIND.

FORGIVENESS CAN HEAL YOUR SOUL.

FORGIVENESS CAN HEAL YOUR SPIRIT.

FORGIVENESS CAN SAVE YOUR LOVED ONES!

God's part is to forgive when you forgive those who have sinned against you, so let's

FORGIVE AND FORGET RIGHT NOW!

Hebrews 10:18 (KJV) says our sins are *"forever forgiven and forgotten!"* Hallelujah!

FORGIVENESS LEADS TO THIS WAY UP!

THIS WAY UP!

Is it possible to stay "up" all the time?

YES!!!

Is it possible for everyone to stay "up" all the time?

YES!!!

Is it possible for even ME to stay "up" all the time?

YES!!!

How?

Do what this book says, because we've told you how to find

THIS WAY UP!